PROBLEMS IN EUROPEAN CIVILIZATION

UNDER THE EDITORIAL DIRECTION OF

Ralph W. Greenlaw and Dwight E. Lee†*

Other volumes in preparation

THE INDUSTRIAL REVOLUTION
IN BRITAIN

Triumph or Disaster?

PROBLEMS IN EUROPEAN CIVILIZATION

THE
INDUSTRIAL REVOLUTION
IN BRITAIN

Triumph or Disaster?

EDITED WITH AN INTRODUCTION BY

Philip A. M. Taylor

UNIVERSITY OF BIRMINGHAM, ENGLAND

D. C. HEATH AND COMPANY · BOSTON

Library of Congress Catalog Card number 58-12573

Copyright © 1958 by D. C. Heath and Company

*No part of the material covered by this copyright may be reproduced
in any form without written permission of the publisher.* (6 L 4)

PRINTED IN THE UNITED STATES OF AMERICA

Table of Contents

Introduction

Everyone agrees that in the century 1750–1850 there took place in Britain economic changes of great importance. A variety of technical innovations, their application to bring about a vast increase in industrial production, the location of industry in new concentrations, an increase in the volume of overseas trade, a rapid growth in the proportion of the population living in cities — all these were features of the period. While the 1851 Census did not deal with production, it showed not only that British population had doubled in half a century, not only that the population of industrial cities had increased far more rapidly, but that for the first time in history a large state had half its population living in towns.[1] All this is fact. But historians desire to ask further questions. Did the changes of this century, or any part of it, constitute anything that can properly be called "The Industrial Revolution"? In other words, was there anything especially sudden or violent about them, and were they of unique significance in British economic history, or were they merely one set of rapid changes among others that history could show? Second, what was the effect of these economic changes, however we describe them, on the standard of life of the mass of the British people? Historians have not agreed on their answers, and to illustrate their controversies a selection has been made from the writings of eleven of them (including the two Hammonds): one German, one French, two American, and seven British; of whom seven are still alive.

While the phrase "Industrial Revolution," or something like it, can be found very early in the nineteenth century, it was given its wide currency by the lectures delivered at Oxford by Arnold Toynbee and published in 1884, after his early death. It was in the eighth of these lectures that Toynbee summed up his views about the period 1750–1850. He pointed out the rapid growth of population; the modernization both of the techniques and of the organization of farming, especially the transforming, by the process of enclosure, of medieval open fields into modern compact farms; the rapidity of invention in industry, above all in textiles; the development of powerful machines and their grouping into factories. To him, these changes seemed emphatically revolutionary. But he thought he saw, in addition to these material changes, a change of outlook, from the medieval desire to regulate economic life to a modern acceptance of free competition. He considered that for the lower classes in town and country the total result was disastrous. "Production on a vast scale," he said at the end of Lecture VII, "the result of free competition, led to a rapid alienation of classes and to the degradation of a large body of producers."[2]

Toynbee's view of the process as a revolution is by no means dead. Not only is it still the popular view, but so well-balanced a scholar as H. L. Beales could say in 1928: "The industrial revolution replaced one so-

[1] By 1881, the date of the last Census Toynbee could use, the proportion was about two thirds; it is now about nine tenths. The United States first recorded a half-urban population at the Census of 1920.

[2] Arnold Toynbee, *Lectures on the Industrial Revolution in England* (1884), p. 84.

cial system or civilization by another."[3] The views of the French historian Mantoux were similar: there were preparatory stages, to be sure, but in the later eighteenth century there was a "decisive crisis," a transformation so complete that, after the very early nineteenth century, economic developments, however large, were only the "working out of the drama" after the stage had been set. In that transformation, he singled out as central the emergence of the factory as the typical unit of production, and the consequent separation of society into two clearly distinguished, and even mutually hostile classes, the owners and the workers.[4] But this judgment has been challenged from two sides.

On the one hand, it has been argued that earlier industrial progress in Britain was so great that the developments of the late eighteenth century represented no unique change. A few years ago, Professor Nef began a book with the words: "There have been two industrial revolutions in England, not one."[5] The second reading is an article in which he states his conclusions and presents a selection from the supporting evidence. In the main, the facts must be accepted, though the scale of production described is often surprisingly small. But the conclusions need to be thought out carefully. Did the developments Nef describes amount to a transformation of industry, or of society, comparable to that which occurred between 1750 and 1850? Or was the early eighteenth century, as pictured in Defoe's *Tour Through England and Wales* for example, still very like the Britain of Henry VIII?

On the other hand, the transformation of society, or even of industry, was by no means complete in 1830 or 1850. This has best been brought out in the monumental study by Sir John Clapham, who, incidentally, never uses the words "industrial revolution." From the very long chapters dealing with this theme, the reading chosen concerns the major textile industries, which have always, and rightly, been singled out as being the first industries to be transformed, and which dominated British export trade until late in the nineteenth century. The picture Clapham presents is one of old and new stages of technique and organization existing side by side. Other sectors of British economic life were far less "revolutionized." There were more shoemakers than either coalminers or woolen workers, as Clapham points out elsewhere, and as many domestic servants as workers in cottons, woolens, and silks combined; there were more blacksmiths than makers of iron; and one-quarter of all men over twenty got their living from agriculture.[6]

Even if all this is admitted, it is still possible to argue, with Mantoux, that one stage of development was more "decisive" than another. But however you decide that question, Toynbee's second theme remains to be discussed, and the bulk of the present readings are concerned with this. A foreigner reading the obvious books about the comparable period of American industrialization is impressed by the fact that complaints against capitalists are based so much on their alleged connection with political corruption, their ruthless attacks on the interests of smaller businessmen, and their exploitation of the consuming public. American readers of British books on the Industrial Revolution will probably be equally impressed by their overwhelming emphasis on the sufferings inflicted by capitalists on the workers.

At the time, the most influential people in Britain were optimistic. Many of them thought that social improvement could not result from state intervention. But they

[3] Henry L. Beales, *The Industrial Revolution, 1750–1850. An Introductory Essay* (1928), p. 4.

[4] Paul Mantoux, *The Industrial Revolution of the Eighteenth Century* (1928 English edition: the first French edition was 1906), pp. 27, 43, 57.

[5] John U. Nef, *Industry and Government in France and Britain, 1540–1640* (Philadelphia, 1940), p. 1.

[6] John H. Clapham, *An Economic History of Modern Britain*, Vol. II, *Free Trade and Steel* (Cambridge, 1932), pp. 21–5. The figures are from the 1851 Census.

usually thought that economic progress would, in the not too distant future, result in social benefits for all. *The Economist,* on May 3, 1851, commented thus on the Great Exhibition that had just been opened:

The Queen of the mightiest empire of the globe — the empire in which industry is the most successfully cultivated, and in which its triumphs have been greatest — was fittingly occupied in consecrating the temple erected to its honour. . . . The contrast and the change we have noticed — the present devotion to peace, and the former appliance to war, telling of a future still more peaceful than the present — the former disdain of political power for humble industry, and the present honour it bestows, telling of a future when the hand or the skill of the labourer shall be held in still higher honour . . . are convincing proofs of the moral improvement already made; and they give us irresistible assurances that a yet higher destiny awaits our successors even on earth.

But already the Chartist movement had combined many forms of protest. Already in 1848 the Communist Manifesto had been written, with its emphatic statement that under capitalism the worker "becomes an appendage of the machine." In 1867 there was to appear the first installment of the major work of Communist theory, Karl Marx's *Capital.*

Marx was writing a theoretical analysis of capitalism as an intellectual proof of something he had already decided in his own mind: that capitalism was evil, that it was approaching obsolescence, and that the oppressed proletariat, when conscious of its situation as a class, could and would rise to overthrow it and substitute a new social order. The description of the growth of capitalism is a rather small part of the book. But what he wrote is interesting. Like his partner Engels, Marx was deeply impressed by the industrialization of Britain.[7] At

times, they both concentrated on the conditions of their own day, and found them vile. But in this full-scale historical treatment, Marx writes of the development of capitalism as a very long process, resulting from the interplay of many forces. Here, the period 1750–1850 is seen as only a part of a larger story. Marx, of course, was in no doubt as to the deplorable effects of capitalist development on the mass of the population. But in *Capital* he describes the fate of the proletariat as the result of the entire system of capitalism, in its early phases of commercial expansion and domestic system in industry as well as in its mechanized factory stage. Finally, in Marx's view, the whole process was not purely economic in character. The class that was achieving dominance, he claimed, used the state as its instrument to increase and maintain its power, and the reading here presented illustrates this view.

Many later writers have seemed to agree with Marx's views, as regards nineteenth century social conditions, though they were writing history and not trying to shape proletarian class-consciousness.[8] Yet, from Toynbee on, they tended to neglect the earlier period of capitalist development. These points are illustrated in the works of Dr. and Mrs. Hammond, who have been far more influential than Marx in molding the popular British view of history. In addition to a brilliant biography of Lord Shaftesbury, they have written five major books on working-class conditions in the period of the Industrial Revolution, and to the Hammonds the word "Revolution" has full force. Scientific triumphs, they agree, were achieved, and new opportunities for enterprise appeared. But these opportunities were open only to the man who "was prepared to work like a slave and to live

---

[7] Books and government reports on the Industrial Revolution in Britain formed most of the raw material for Marx's theories. It is encouraging — or frightening — to the student to know that the history of the world can be changed by the interpretation, or the misunderstanding, of what we are here discussing.

[8] Like Toynbee, however, they have often been reformers. It is interesting to note that modern town-planners have taken the same view. The section headings of Chapter 4 of Lewis Mumford's *Technics and Civilization,* include "The New Barbarism," "The Destruction of Environment," "The Degradation of the Worker," and "The Starvation of Life."

like a slave-master."[9] For the worker, they assert, the result was a disaster, for the Industrial Revolution turned "the discomfort of the life of the poor into a rigid system."[10] It was not just that wages were low and hours excessively long. The workers lived in towns, which were "not the refuge of a civilization but the barracks of an industry."[11] They were "treadmill cities where the daylight never broke upon the beauty and the wisdom of the world."[12] The reading from *The Rise of Modern Industry* represents their mature opinion.

A special aspect of the damage alleged to have been done to British society by the Industrial Revolution is the fate of the small landowner, or "yeoman," the small tenant, and the farm-labourer. The Hammonds have written many pages on the injustices of enclosure by Act of Parliament. They have deplored the fact that agricultural production rose at the cost of the destruction of a self-reliant peasantry. They have been much concerned to attack the ruling class, a class of men who practised the rule of law and allowed wide freedom of conduct among themselves, but who were capable of ruthless repression of their social inferiors. "That class has left bright and ample records of its life in literature, in art, in political traditions, in the display of great orations and debates, in memories of brilliant conversation and sparkling wit; it has left dim and meagre records of the disinherited peasants that are the shadow of its wealth; of the exiled labourers that are the shadow of its pleasures; of the villages sinking in poverty and crime and shame that are the shadow of its power and its pride."[13] The reading selected, however,

is from Mantoux. He is habitually temperate in his judgments, and he describes as well as criticizes the process of rural change. Briefly, the argument runs that in the eighteenth century a technical revolution occurred in farming; that this could be applied in common practice only through the destruction of the older system; that this was forced through by the exercise of political power, particularly in the parliamentary enclosures; but that what was destroyed was not merely a system of production but a way of life; and that the dispossessed peasants sank into proletarian status or even pauperism on the land or, displaced from the land altogether, became a reserve of labor at the disposal of the industrialists. This social dislocation, to quote another writer, was "the heavy price which the nation ultimately paid for the supply of bread and meat to its manufacturing population."[14]

Upon these views of the Industrial Revolution's effects in town and country, scholars in our own day have launched a vigorous attack. They have insisted upon the variety of conditions, as between sections of the working class, and between agricultural regions. They emphasize short-period fluctuations, the "trade cycle," and, like Professor Rostow, suggest that what made the age of the Chartists an era of such memorable discontent was the fact that upon the fundamental dislocations of the process of industrialization there was superimposed, in a single decade, the shock of three industrial depressions. They emphasize the practical difficulties of the early industrialists, saying, for example, that what brought about the institution of truck, that is to say the payment of wages in goods rather than hard cash, was less a desire to cheat than the acute shortage of capital. They allege, with Professor Ash-

[9] John L. and Barbara Hammond, *The Town Labourer, 1760–1832, The New Civilization* (1918), p. 8.

[10] *Ibid.*, p. 19.

[11] *Ibid.*, p. 39.

[12] *The Age of the Chartists, 1832–54* (1930), p. 365.

[13] *The Village Labourer, 1760–1832, A Study of the Government of England before the Reform Bill* (1911), p. 332. Enclosure procedure is treated in chapters 3 and 4, with an Appendix

giving case studies. See also chapters 10 and 11, in *The Town Labourer*, "The Mind of the Rich" and "The Conscience of the Rich."

[14] Rowland E. Prothero (Lord Ernle), *English Farming Past and Present* (4th edition, 1927: the first was in 1912), p. 149.

ton, that many hardships should be blamed, not upon industrialization as such, but upon the long wars waged against the French Revolutionaries and Napoleon. As compared with the Hammonds, they tend to minimize state action, except as an occasional hindrance to economic progress. They conclude that, in the long run especially, industrialization was an immense gain for everyone, the workers included.

Such modern revisions are due in part to changes in knowledge of evidence. The use of local records, by J. D. Chambers and others, is noteworthy. The use of the records of business firms is beginning, and we can hope soon to change the present situation, in which so much less is known about the Victorian businessman than about farm-laborers, miners, spinners, and, above all, handloom weavers. More fundamentally, there has been a change in the type of evidence looked for. Professor Ashton suggests that historians have been misled by their reliance upon the official inquiries of the nineteenth century, whose purpose was to expose abuses rather than to describe the entire economic system in normal working order. The use of administrative documents, whether of the state or business firms or landed estates, rather than of contemporary literary sources, similarly reduces the importance in historians' minds of the sensational elements in a social situation.

But other elements, besides the opening up of new evidence, or the reduced reliance upon some types of old, have entered into the revision of traditional judgments. The gross evils which, however caused, certainly existed in the nineteenth century, and among which the early economic historians lived, are no longer with us: British historians do not, in the same sense as Toynbee, need to be humanitarians and reformers. We have become far more conscious of the dislocating effects of war. We are more willing to recognize that economic forces may be more powerful than government policies, even welfare state policies. Preoccupied as we are with the problem of "undeveloped areas," we are more respectful towards the role of the entrepreneur. In a densely populated country and in a competitive world, British thinkers have become more interested in the production of wealth and somewhat less in its distribution.[15] Such insights, derived from the experience of his own world, are not to be rejected by the historian. But even then the factors have not been completely listed. Economic history has come closer — Professor Ashton thinks still not close enough — to economics. Hence historians are coming to think less of government policies, social institutions, classes, and the like, and more of statistics, trends of various lengths, interrelations between the many factors in the growth of firms, industries, or national economies. Rostow's interpretation of the relationship between the trade cycle, harvests, and politics is an example of this approach.

We shall continue to need fresh evidence, for there are many obscurities in the history of the eighteenth and nineteenth centuries. But it is not to be expected that controversy will end as knowledge increases, nor that present insights will be final. For some of the controversy concerns the very nature of what is relevant to economic history as a study.

Some historians have simply tried to present all the facts, with a minimum of generalization and an avoidance of most kinds of judgment. Clapham, for example, reacts against extremes of description of workers' hardships, because he believes them to be based on insufficient evidence; but he devotes several chapters to living conditions, and touches on most of the Hammonds' subject matter, within the nineteenth century.

Second, there are historians who wish to clothe the facts with more meaning, and who profess to find their guiding concepts

[15] Somewhat similar changes have occurred in the views of many American historians regarding the role of early capitalists, with emphasis on their constructive rather than on their predatory characteristics. Contrast Ida Tarbell and Allan Nevins on John D. Rockefeller.

in economic theory. Such men will stress the "impersonal" forces in economic history, will think of correlation between facts and figures, will study long and short fluctuations.[16] They will tend to be especially interested in the causes of the Industrial Revolution, and in its growth, rather than in its social effects. They will tend to regard as irrelevant to their subject all questions of personal aspiration, all class attitudes, and will tend to minimize the importance, in determining economic development, of reform movements and government action. They may be tempted to say that what the Hammonds study should be a separate subject, "social history" perhaps; though this would probably mean that economic history would lose much of its variety and humanity, while the new subject would lack intellectual precision.

Against either of these attitudes, the Hammonds and their supporters have chosen to study the causes of working-class discontent and movements of protest. *The Village Labourer* explored the background of the risings of 1830 in the South of England; *The Town Labourer,* that of the early trade unions; *The Skilled Labourer,* that of the Luddite movement; while the title *The Age of the Chartists* explains itself. For them, living standards have included, not merely hours and wages and costs, but housing and education and open space for recreation. They have been affronted, not merely by the facts of child labor or harsh factory discipline, but by the attitude of rulers who could defend the horrors of their time in the name of reason, progress, and even religion. They have been concerned, in short, not only with physical sufferings but with spiritual deprivation. What is more, they have brought forward evidence to suggest that the workers themselves were interested, not only in material standards, but in status as human beings. " 'The poor man,' said a working-class paper, 'is

esteemed only as an instrument of wealth' " — that is perhaps the centre of their view of the Industrial Revolution.[17] This may have led them to distort the picture, by neglecting some facts and points of view. But in two respects they have held to their convictions with special tenacity. Replying to critics in 1930, Dr. Hammond remarked approvingly of Toynbee that he "lived in a wider and deeper world than the world he was describing."[18] He said also that working-class discontent in the early nineteenth century was "a revolt of the imagination . . . , hostility to a view of life which outraged the poor man's self-respect and gave to his higher wants no place at all in its values."[19] The Hammonds, in short, have continued to claim that historians of periods of economic change should not limit their view too narrowly to technicalities, but should be willing also to consider the non-material elements of life, and even to make judgments in the light of eternal principles.

It is for you to decide which of these ways of studying history is the most defensible. It is for you to decide whether the facts presented in these readings are adequate to support the generalizations, and whether the authors' reasoning is cogent. It is for you to decide, even, whether these long controversies have been fruitful. Certainly it will now be clear that history, as thought about by scholars, is not only a body of agreed fact — which is what "history" as a subject at school commonly amounts to — but is also a complex of doubts, interpretations, and judgments which may vary from time to time, and from one honest and learned man to another.

There is, perhaps, also a more practical value to be derived from this work. In our lifetime, many nations are likely to undergo the experience of industrialization. History

[16] See, for example, Thomas S. Ashton, "The Industrial Revolution," *Economic History Review* ("Studies in Bibliography"), V, No. 1 (1934), esp. p. 116.

[17] *The Town Labourer,* p. 328.
[18] John L. Hammond, "The Industrial Revolution and Discontent," *Economic History Review,* II, No. 2 (1930). p. 220.
[19] *Ibid.,* pp. 227–8.

seems to show that all nations find in this experience many common, perhaps unavoidable, features. But clear thinking about the well-known history of British industrialization may aid in the formulation, by such of today's students as come to exert public influence, of policies which will spare the countries at present "undeveloped" some of the more painful trials which our readings have described.

A Note on Procedure

It has been my aim to choose readings from reputable historians. While I have had to omit many details, I have chosen the longest possible continuous passages, and I have never changed the order of an argument. To save space, however, I have omitted the authors' footnotes, for the detailed references to original sources, inaccessible to most students, are sometimes almost as long as the text. Anyone wishing to study the Industrial Revolution seriously will have to read many of the works listed in "Suggestions for Additional Reading." In them he will find all the documentation he can possibly enjoy.

GLOSSARY

No attempt has been made to annotate names of authors mentioned in the readings, nor to provide a substitute for a map of Britain. The aim is merely to explain such technical terms as may not be clearly defined in the readings, and could probably not be found in a dictionary.

BLUE BOOKS   Colloquial term for the reports of British Royal Commissions or Select Committees.

CHARTIST MOVEMENT   Movement of working men in Britain, active between 1837 and 1848. Its immediate aims were embodied in The People's Charter, with six points: the vote for all men, vote by secret ballot, constituencies of equal population, re-election of the House of Commons every year, abolition of property qualifications for Members of Parliament, and payment of salaries to Members. The reformed House of Commons would, it was hoped, initiate sweeping social reforms.

CIVIL WAR   Conflict between King and Parliament which continued, with intervals, from 1642 to 1651.

COMMON FIELD SYSTEM   Form of agricultural organization, lasting in parts of Britain and Europe from the Middle Ages to the nineteenth century. A village had large fields, often three, undivided by hedges or ditches. Within these, cultivators held their land in small scattered strips. Property-holding was individual, but the planning of crops, grazing, etc., involved much community regulation.

COMMONS (or WASTE)   That portion of land in a village which was permanent natural pasture, on which villagers could graze their livestock in numbers roughly proportional to their arable holdings in the open fields.

CONSOLS   British Government securities.

COPYHOLDER   Villager who held his land "by copy of court roll," a tenure of late medieval origin, and very common in the sixteenth, seventeenth, and eighteenth centuries. Such a man was not an owner, but his rent was more or less fixed — not subject to periodic review, as with a lease — and the tenure was hereditary, either indefinitely or for a stated number of generations, on payment of a "fine" at each succession of an heir.

CORN LAWS   For present purposes, a series of laws dating from the late seventeenth century, and especially the law of 1815, relating to all grains. The aim was to maintain stable, and usually high, prices for producers. The methods commonly employed were to prohibit the sale of imported grain when home prices were below a stated level (thus eighty shillings a quarter for wheat in 1815), to grant a bounty on exports of grain when home prices were very low, and, occasionally, to prohibit exports of grain when prices at home were unduly high.

DISSOLUTION OF MONASTERIES   Policy of Henry VIII, carried out in two stages, 1536 and 1539.

DOMESTIC SYSTEM Form of industrial organization, in which people worked in their own homes with hand-operated machinery often owned by themselves. Their material was distributed to them, and their product was collected from them for marketing, by a capitalist, who therefore became in large measure their employer, though he exerted no detailed supervision or discipline of the factory type.

FARMER In British usage, a tenant, *not* an owner. But often a man with a holding of one, two, or three hundred acres.

GUILD (today commonly spelled **GILD**) Medieval organization of independent masters in a single craft. Their purpose in forming a gild was partly economic, to supervise workmanship but above all to restrict the numbers practising the craft; partly social, a primitive and local form of social security.

LUDDITE MOVEMENT Movement of protest against the factory system, taking the form of destruction of machinery, especially in the year 1812.

NEW POOR LAW The Act of 1834, administered by local Boards of Guardians elected by the more prosperous inhabitants. The sick, disabled, etc., could receive relief at home. But the able-bodied recipients had to live in workhouses, under conditions, including separation of the sexes, designed to be "less eligible" than any encountered in paid employment.

OPEN FIELD SYSTEM Synonym for **COMMON FIELD SYSTEM**, q.v.

OUTWORK SYSTEM Synonym for **DOMESTIC SYSTEM**, q.v. Sometimes also called the Putting-out System.

REFORM ACT As used in the period being studied, the Act of 1832. This abolished the parliamentary representation of many small boroughs, granting it instead to large industrial cities. It also set up a uniform franchise in boroughs which, while still confined to the middle class, extended the right to vote to several hundred thousand new people.

SPEENHAMLAND SYSTEM System of poor relief adopted by the Berkshire Justices of the Peace, meeting at Speenhamland in 1795, and widely copied. The paying of money from the rates was permitted, to supplement wages up to a fixed figure, when the price of bread reached a level regarded as imposing hardship on workers. The system was swept away by the Act of 1834.

STOCKINGER Domestic worker, making woolen stockings, especially in the East Midlands.

TITHE Proportion of crops and livestock, or their money equivalent, paid by cultivators for the support of the Established Church.

YEOMAN A colloquial rather than a technical expression, common in the sixteenth, seventeenth, and eighteenth centuries. It usually meant a freeholder, owning land on a modest scale, self-supporting but with no pretensions to gentility. Such a man often held local offices, below the rank of Justice of the Peace, and, if his holding was worth forty shillings or more a year, he could vote in parliamentary elections.

The Conflict of Opinion

The traditional view of social change caused by the "Industrial Revolution," if the expression may be used:

> "In the early days of competition the capitalists used all their power to oppress the labourers, and drove down wages to starvation point."
>
> — ARNOLD TOYNBEE

To which a modern reply is:

> "If harvests had been uniformly good; if statesmen had directed their attention to providing a stable standard of value and a proper medium of exchange; if there had been no wars to force up prices, raise rates of interest, and turn resources to destruction, the course of the industrial revolution would have been smoother, and its consequences would not have been, as they are, in doubt."
>
> — THOMAS S. ASHTON

The traditional view on the small landholders:

> "Industry was the only refuge of thousands of men who found themselves cut off from their traditional occupations. The manufacturers were to offer them the living they could no longer earn on the land."
>
> — PAUL MANTOUX

But a modern local historian asserts:

> "At some time in the eighteenth century the movement of population had taken an upward turn in village and town alike and provided an entirely new supply of human material beside which the dislocations caused by enclosure were of secondary importance."
>
> — JONATHAN D. CHAMBERS

Of the working class, an economist says:

> "The most serious unrest was a product of cyclical depression and high food prices."
>
> — WALT WHITMAN ROSTOW

But humanitarian historians reply that much more than material sufferings were involved:

> "In adapting this new power to the satisfaction of its wants England could not escape from the moral atmosphere of the slave trade: the atmosphere in which it was the fashion to think of men as things. . . . The age had turned aside from making a society in order to make a system of production."
>
> — JOHN L. and BARBARA HAMMOND

THE CLASSICAL DEFINITION OF THE INDUSTRIAL REVOLUTION

ARNOLD TOYNBEE

Arnold Toynbee died in 1883, at the age of thirty-one. But although the volume of lectures, from which the following excerpt is taken, was his only published work, his influence was unusually great. Toynbee was deeply interested in working-class conditions. He was critical of the dogmas of nineteenth-century economics. He was eager to reform the Church of England, especially in the direction of greater influence for the laity. But he did not subscribe to the doctrines of any brand of socialism. He was a member of no organized movement. He was simply a man whose personality and ideas made a profound impression on his contemporaries at Oxford, most of whom lived into the present century. The study of economic history, the more democratic organization of the Church, educational movements among adult workers, and the famous settlement in the East End of London, all acknowledge some debt to Toynbee.

THE ESSENCE of the Industrial Revolution is the substitution of competition for the medieval regulations which had previously controlled the production and distribution of wealth. On this account it is not only one of the most important facts of English history, but Europe owes to it the growth of two great systems of thought — Economic Science, and its antithesis, Socialism. The development of Economic Science in England has four chief landmarks, each connected with the name of one of the four great English economists. The first is the publication of Adam Smith's *Wealth of Nations* in 1776, in which he investigated the causes of wealth and aimed at the substitution of industrial freedom for a system of restriction. The production of wealth, not the welfare of man, was what Adam Smith had primarily before his mind's eye; in his own words, "the great

object of the Political Economy of every country is to increase the riches and power of that country." His great book appeared on the eve of the Industrial Revolution. A second stage in the growth of the science is marked by Malthus's *Essay on Population,* published in 1798, which may be considered the product of that revolution, then already in full swing. Adam Smith had concentrated all his attention on a large production; Malthus directed his inquiries, not to the causes of wealth but to the causes of poverty, and found them in his theory of population. A third stage is marked by Ricardo's *Principles of Political Economy and Taxation* which appeared in 1817, and in which Ricardo sought to ascertain the laws of the distribution of wealth. Adam Smith had shown how wealth could be produced under a system of industrial freedom, Ricardo showed how wealth is dis-

From Arnold Toynbee, *Lectures on the Industrial Revolution* (Rivington, 1884). Lecture VIII, pp. 85–93.

tributed under such a system, a problem which could not have occurred to any one before his time. The fourth stage is marked by John Stuart Mill's *Principles of Political Economy*, published in 1848. Mill himself asserted that "the chief merit of his treatise" was the distinction drawn between the laws of production and those of distribution, and the problem he tried to solve was, how wealth *ought to be* distributed. A great advance was made by Mill's attempt to show what was and what was not inevitable under a system of free competition. In it we see the influence which the rival system of Socialism was already beginning to exercise upon the economists. The whole spirit of Mill's book is quite different from that of any economic works which had up to his time been written in England. Though a re-statement of Ricardo's system, it contained the admission that the distribution of wealth is the result of "particular social arrangements," and it recognized that competition alone is not a satisfactory basis of society.

Competition, heralded by Adam Smith, and taken for granted by Ricardo and Mill, is still the dominant idea of our time; though since the publication of the *Origin of Species*, we hear more of it under the name of the "struggle for existence." I wish here to notice the fallacies involved in the current arguments on this subject. In the first place it is assumed that all competition is a competition for existence. This is not true. There is a great difference between a struggle for mere existence and a struggle for a particular kind of existence. For instance, twelve men are struggling for employment in a trade where there is only room for eight; four are driven out of that trade, but they are not trampled out of existence. A good deal of competition merely decides what kind of work a man is to do; though of course when a man can only do one kind of work, it may easily become a struggle for bare life. It is next assumed that this struggle for existence is a law of nature, and that therefore all human interference with it is wrong. To that I answer that the whole meaning of civilization is interference with this brute struggle. We intend to modify the violence of the fight, and to prevent the weak being trampled under foot.

Competition, no doubt, has its uses. Without competition no progress would be possible, for progress comes chiefly from without; it is external pressure which forces men to exert themselves. Socialists, however, maintain that this advantage is gained at the expense of an enormous waste of human life and labour, which might be avoided by regulation. But here we must distinguish between competition in production and competition in distribution, a difference recognized in modern legislation, which has widened the sphere of contract in the one direction, while it has narrowed it in the other. For the struggle of men to outvie one another in production is beneficial to the community; their struggle over the division of the joint produce is not. The stronger side will dictate its own terms; and as a matter of fact, in the early days of competition the capitalists used all their power to oppress the labourers, and drove down wages to starvation point. This kind of competition has to be checked; there is no historical instance of its having lasted long without being modified either by combination or legislation, or both. In England both remedies are in operation, the former through Trades-Unions, the latter through factory legislation. In the past other remedies were applied. It is this desire to prevent the evils of competition that affords the true explanation of the fixing of wages by Justices of the Peace, which seemed to Ricardo a remnant of the old system of tyranny in the interests of the strong. Competition, we have now learnt, is neither good nor evil in itself; it is a force which has to be studied and controlled; it may be compared to a stream whose strength and direction have to be observed, that embankments may be thrown up within which it may do its work harmlessly and beneficially. But at the period we are considering it came to be believed in as a gospel, and, the idea of necessity being superadded, economic laws deduced from the assumption of universal unrestricted competition were converted into practical precepts, from which it was regarded as little short of immoral to depart.

Coming to the facts of the Industrial Revolution, the first thing that strikes us is the far greater rapidity which marks the growth of population. Before 1751 the largest decennial increase, so far as we can calculate from our imperfect materials, was 3 per cent. For each of the next three decennial periods the increase was 6 per cent; then between 1781 and 1791 it was 9 per cent; between 1791 and 1801, 11 per cent; between 1801 and 1811, 14 per cent; between 1811 and 1821, 18 per cent. This is the highest figure ever reached in England, for since 1815 a vast emigration has been always tending to moderate it; between 1815 and 1880 over eight millions (including Irish) have left our shores. But for this our normal rate of increase would be 16 or 18 instead of 12 per cent in every decade.

Next we notice the relative and positive decline in the agricultural population. In 1811 it constituted 35 per cent of the whole population of Great Britain; in 1821, 33 per cent; in 1831, 28 per cent. And at the same time its actual numbers have decreased. In 1831 there were 1,243,057 adult males employed in agriculture in Great Britain; in 1841 there were 1,207,989. In 1851 the whole number of persons engaged in agriculture in England was 2,084,153; in 1861 it was 2,010,454, and in 1871 it was 1,657,138. Contemporaneously with this change, the centre of density of population has shifted from the Midlands to the North; there are at the present day 458 persons to the square mile in the counties north of the Trent, as against 312 south of the Trent. And we have lastly to remark the change in the relative population of England and Ireland. Of the total population of the three kingdoms, Ireland had in 1821 32 per cent, in 1881 only 14.6 per cent.

An agrarian revolution plays as large a part in the great industrial change of the end of the eighteenth century as does the revolution in manufacturing industries, to which attention is more usually directed. Our next inquiry must therefore be: What were the agricultural changes which led to this noticeable decrease in the rural population? The three most effective causes were: the destruction of the common-field system of cultivation; the enclosure, on a large scale, of commons and waste lands; and the consolidation of small farms into large. We have already seen that while between 1710 and 1760 some 300,000 acres were enclosed, between 1760 and 1843 nearly 7,000,000 underwent the same process. Closely connected with the enclosure system was the substitution of large for small farms. In the first half of the century Laurence, though approving of consolidation from an economic point of view, had thought that the odium attaching to an evicting landlord would operate as a strong check upon it. But these scruples had now disappeared. Eden in 1795 notices how constantly the change was effected, often accompanied by the conversion of arable to pasture; and relates how in a certain Dorsetshire village he found two farms where twenty years ago there had been thirty. The process went on uninterruptedly into the present century. Cobbett, writing in 1826, says: "In the parish of Burghclere one single farmer holds, under Lord Carnarvon, as one farm, the lands that those now living remember to have formed fourteen farms, bringing up in a respectable way fourteen families." The consolidation of farms reduced the number of farmers, while the enclosures drove the labourers off the land as it became impossible for them to exist without their rights of pasturage for sheep and geese on common lands.

Severely, however, as these changes bore upon the rural population, they wrought, without doubt, distinct improvement from an agricultural point of view. They meant the substitution of scientific for unscientific culture. "It has been found," says Laurence, "by long experience, that common or open fields are great hindrances to the public good, and to the honest improvement which every one might make of his own." Enclosures brought an extension of arable cultivation and the tillage of inferior soils; and in small farms of 40 to 100 acres, where the land was exhausted by repeated corn crops, the farm buildings of clay and mud walls and three-fourths of the estate often saturated with water, consolidation into farms of 100 to 500 acres meant rotation of crops, leases of nineteen years, and good farm buildings. The period was one of great agricultural advance; the breed of cattle was improved, rotation of crops was generally introduced, the steam-plough was invented, agricultural societies were instituted. In one respect alone the change was injurious. In consequence of the high prices of corn which prevailed during the French war, some of the finest permanent pastures were broken up. Still, in spite of this, it was said in 1813 that during the previous ten years agricultural produce had increased by one-fourth, and this was an increase upon a great increase in the preceding generation.

Passing to manufactures, we find here the all-prominent fact to be the substitution of the factory for the domestic system, the consequence of the mechanical discoveries of the time. Four great inventions altered the character of the cotton manufacture; the spinning-jenny, patented by Hargreaves in 1770; the water-frame, invented by Arkwright the year before; Crompton's mule introduced in 1779, and the self-acting mule, first invented by Kelly in 1792, but not brought into use till Roberts improved it in 1825. None of these by themselves would have revolutionized the industry. But in 1769 — the year in which Napoleon and Wellington were born — James Watt took out his patent for the steam-engine. Sixteen years later it was applied to the cotton manufacture. In 1785 Boulton and Watt made an engine for a cotton-mill at Papplewick in Notts, and in the same year Arkwright's patent expired. These two facts taken together mark the introduction of the factory system. But the

most famous invention of all, and the most fatal to domestic industry, the power-loom, though also patented by Cartwright in 1785, did not come into use for several years, and till the power-loom was introduced the workman was hardly injured. At first, in fact, machinery raised the wages of spinners and weavers owing to the great prosperity it brought to the trade. In fifteen years the cotton trade trebled itself; from 1788 to 1803 has been called "its golden age"; for, before the power-loom but after the introduction of the mule and other mechanical improvements by which for the first time yarn sufficiently fine for muslin and a variety of other fabrics was spun, the demand became such that "old barns, cart-houses, out-buildings of all descriptions were repaired, windows broke through old blank walls, and all fitted up for loom-shops; new weavers' cottages with loom-shops arose in every direction, every family bringing home weekly from 40 to 120 shillings per week." At a later date, the condition of the workman was very different. Meanwhile, the iron industry had been equally revolutionized by the invention of smelting by pit-coal brought into use between 1740 and 1750, and by the application in 1788 of the steam-engine to blast furnaces. In the eight years which followed this latter date, the amount of iron manufactured nearly doubled itself.

A further growth of the factory system took place independent of machinery, and owed its origin to the expansion of trade, an expansion which was itself due to the great advance made at this time in the means of communication. The canal system was being rapidly developed throughout the country. In 1777 the Grand Trunk canal, 96 miles in length, connecting the Trent and Mersey, was finished; Hull and Liverpool were connected by one canal while another connected them both with Bristol; and in 1792, the Grand Junction canal, 90 miles in length, made a water-way from London through Oxford to the chief midland towns. Some years afterwards, the roads were greatly improved under Telford and Macadam; between 1818 and 1829 more than a thousand additional miles of turnpike road were constructed; and the next year, 1830, saw the opening of the first railroad. These improved means of communication caused an extraordinary increase in commerce, and to secure a sufficient supply of goods it became the interest of the merchants to collect weavers around them in great numbers, to get looms together in a workshop, and to give out the warp themselves to the workpeople. To these latter this system meant a change from independence to dependence; at the beginning of the century the report of a committee asserts that the essential difference between the domestic and the factory system is, that in the latter the work is done "by persons who have no property in the goods they manufacture." Another direct consequence of this expansion of trade was the regular recurrence of periods of over-production and of depression, a phenomenon quite unknown under the old system, and due to this new form of production on a large scale for a distant market.

These altered conditions in the production of wealth necessarily involved an equal revolution in its distribution. In agriculture the prominent fact is an enormous rise in rents. Up to 1795, though they had risen in some places, in others they had been stationary since the Revolution. But between 1790 and 1833, according to Porter, they at least doubled. In Scotland, the rental of land, which in 1795 had amounted to £2,000,000, had risen in 1815 to £5,278,-685. A farm in Essex, which before 1793 had been rented at 10 shillings an acre, was let in 1812 at 50 shillings, though, six years after, this had fallen again to 35 shillings. In Berks and Wilts, farms which in 1790 were let at 14s., were let in 1810 at 70s., and in 1820 at 50s. Much of this rise, doubtless, was due to money invested in improvements — the first Lord Leicester is said to have expended £400,000 on his property — but it was far more largely the effect of the enclosure system, of the consolidation of farms, and of the high price of corn during the French war. Whatever may have been its causes, however, it represented a great social revolution, a change in the balance of political power and in the relative position of classes. The farmers shared in the prosperity of the landlords; for many of them held their farms under beneficial leases, and made large profits by them. In consequence, their character completely changed; they ceased to work and live with their labourers, and became a distinct class. The high prices of the war time thoroughly demoralized them, for their wealth then increased so fast, that they were at a loss what to do with it. Cobbett has described the change in their habits, the new food and furniture, the luxury and drinking, which were the consequences of more money coming into their hands than they knew how to spend. Meanwhile, the effect of all these agrarian changes upon the condition of the labourer was an exactly opposite and most disastrous one. He felt all the burden of high prices, while his wages were steadily falling, and he had lost his common-rights. It is from this period, viz., the beginning of the present century, that the alienation between farmer and labourer may be dated.

Exactly analogous phenomena appeared in the manufacturing world. The new class of great capitalist employers made enormous fortunes, they took little or no part personally in the work of their factories, their hundreds of workmen were individually unknown to them; and as a consequence, the old relations between masters and men disappeared, and a "cash nexus" was substituted for the human tie. The workmen on their side resorted to combination, and Trades-Unions began a fight which looked as if it were between mortal enemies rather than joint producers. The misery which came upon large sections of the working people at this epoch was often, though not always, due to a fall in wages, for, as I said above, in some industries they rose. But they suffered likewise from the conditions of labour under the factory system, from the rise of prices, especially from the high price of bread before the repeal of the corn-laws, and from those sudden fluctuations of trade, which, ever since production has been on a large scale, have exposed them to recurrent periods of bitter distress. The effects of the Industrial Revolution prove that free competition may produce wealth without producing well-being. We all know the horrors that ensued in England before it was restrained by legislation and combination.

NOT ONE, BUT TWO INDUSTRIAL REVOLUTIONS

JOHN U. NEF

Now Professor in the University of Chicago, J. U. Nef's early writings were concerned with the details of economic history in Britain and France in the early modern period. His biggest book is *The Growth of the British Coal Industry,* which treats the subject from the Middle Ages to the eighteenth century. He went on to generalize, as in this article, about the speed of industrial development in the years 1540–1640, and concluded that the theory of a catastrophic Industrial Revolution two centuries later was misguided. More recently, Professor Nef has turned to the relationship between warfare and economic development, in *War and Human Progress* (1950).

SINCE Arnold Toynbee gave his famous lectures at Oxford, fifty years ago, closer study has taken from the concept of the "Industrial Revolution" much of its revolutionary character. Nowhere, perhaps, has the revision of earlier notions concerning the period from 1760 to 1832 been more drastic than with respect to the nature and magnitude of the changes in industrial technique and organization. The industrial plant owned by private capitalists, who employed in it dozens and sometimes scores and even hundreds of workmen, was not the novelty it was once believed to be. Evidence has been piling up to prove that large-scale industry, in this sense, was common in mining and many branches of manufacture long before the middle of the eighteenth century. At the same time, more detailed studies of nineteenth century economic history, especially the quantitative survey of Professor Clapham, have shown that earlier writers, with their eyes focussed upon cotton and iron and upon the most advanced industrial areas, have exaggerated the place of the steam-engine and of large-scale industry in the economy of the eighteen-thirties.

But it is still common to regard the sixties and seventies of the eighteenth century as an important historical boundary, in the sense that there began at this time the first great speeding up of industrial development. If Toynbee had lived to reply to some of the criticisms of the phrase "Industrial Revolution," he might have defended his position by referring to the passage in Macaulay's celebrated third chapter — which may possibly have influenced him during his short life — where Macaulay says that about the middle of the eighteenth century economic progress became for the first time "portentously rapid." But was this the first period of English history in which a remarkable speeding up of industrial development occurred? The opinion is gain-

From John U. Nef, "The Progress of Technology and the Growth of Large-Scale Industry in Great Britain, 1540–1640," *The Economic History Review*, V. No. 1 (1934), pp. 3–15, 16–20, 22–4. By permission of the author and *The Economic History Review*. [The views advanced in this selection by Professor Nef have been substantially developed in Chapter II of his *Cultural Foundations of Industrial Civilization* (The Wiles Lectures II), published by the Cambridge University Press.]

ing strength that there was at least one earlier period during which the rate of change was scarcely less striking. The period begins at about the time of the dissolution of the monasteries, and the industrial development becomes most rapid during the latter half of Elizabeth's reign and in the reign of James I. The forces of rapid change then set in motion continue throughout the seventeenth and eighteenth centuries, but it is not until the second half of the eighteenth century that the pace again becomes as fast as it had been during Shakespeare's lifetime.

Support for this view of industrial history is to be found in the excellent book of Mr. Wadsworth and Miss Mann on the cotton textile industry. It is there suggested that the growth of an elaborate network of middlemen, who supplied the materials upon which thousands of domestic workpeople laboured at their spinning-wheels or looms, was so remarkable in the late sixteenth and early seventeenth centuries that the changes in the face of industrial Lancashire were scarcely less important than between 1760 and 1832, when the county was the classic home of the "revolution" in cotton manufacture. Evidence of an enormous expansion, beginning about the middle of the sixteenth century, in the output of coal, salt, glass, and ships, and of a great increase in the production of many other industrial commodities, such as alum, soap, gunpowder, metal goods, and accessories, will be found in my book on the coal industry. The growth in the importance of mining and manufacturing in the national economy was, it seems, scarcely less rapid between the middle of the sixteenth century and the Civil War than between the middle of the eighteenth century and the first Reform Act. Some other results of recent research seem to indicate that the rapid growth of industry, and the striking increase in the importance and complexity of the domestic system, which began in the Elizabethan Age, were accompanied by equally remarkable changes in industrial technique and scale of enterprise.

Three kinds of technical development helped the growth of large-scale industry between 1540 and 1640. The first was the introduction of capitalistic industries which had scarcely gained a foothold in Great Britain before the Reformation. The second was the application to old industries of various technical processes known before, especially in some districts on the Continent, but hitherto very little used in Great Britain. The third was the discovery and application of new technical methods. It is necessary to consider each of these before turning to other factors which also stimulated the growth of large-scale industry.

1. THE INTRODUCTION OF "NEW" INDUSTRIES

During the last sixty years of the sixteenth century the first paper and gunpowder mills, the first cannon foundries, the first alum and copperas factories, the first sugar refineries, and the first considerable saltpetre works were all introduced into the country from abroad. The discovery of calamine, the ore of zinc, in Somerset and elsewhere, together with the first really effective attempts to mine copper ore, made possible the establishment of brass-making and battery works for hammering brass and copper ingots into plates. Not all the commodities turned out by these manufactures were being produced in England for the first time. But the quantities had been insignificant, the plant for producing them primitive. The first important thing about the "new" Elizabethan industries was that in all of them plant was set up involving investments far beyond the sums which groups of master-craftsmen could muster, even if these artisans were men of some small substance. While in London, Sheffield, or any provincial town, the typical workshop of the smith, the cutler, or the weaver could be equipped with its forge or grinding wheel or loom and other necessary tools for a few pounds, the establishments erected in these new industries cost hundreds, and in many cases thousands, of pounds. A further heavy outlay had to be made on materials and labour, because the process of production frequently required a long time, and it was many months before any return could be expected from sales.

In the reign of James I, the alum houses near Whitby, on the Yorkshire coast, were great wooden structures. Each contained large brick furnaces and cisterns, piles of alumstone, coal and wood fuel, and about ten metal pans for boiling the ingredients. Many thousands of pounds had been spent on each of them, and the annual expense of the materials consumed in the manufacture exceeded £1,000. In the reign of Charles I, the copperas house at Queensborough in Kent, with its great wooden troughs, leaden pipes, and cisterns, was built on a similar scale. In 1613, John Browne, later Crown commissioner for making ordnance and shot, and official gunmaker to the Parliament in the Civil War, employed 200 men in his cannon foundry at Brenchley in Kent. At Dartford, in the same county, a paper mill had been set up by John Spilman, a naturalized German, about the middle of Elizabeth's reign. The enterprise certainly employed scores of hands. One of the two great water-wheels which drove the hammers for beating the cloth and the stamping machinery had formerly been used to drive the bellows of a blast-furnace on the same site, and the cost of converting it to its new purpose is said to have been between £1,400 and £1,500. Powder mills, introduced in Surrey just after the middle of the sixteenth century, were also driven by waterpower, and the machinery was perhaps no less costly than at the paper-mills. In addition, there were at least two other elaborately equipped buildings at a powder factory — the corning house and the stove, a separate establishment about twenty feet square in which the powder was dried, the whole room being heated to the proper temperature by an iron fireplace. The battery works introduced from Germany in Elizabeth's reign, with their furnaces and numerous great hammers, some of which weighed 500 pounds, probably cost as much as the larger paper and powder mills. The hammers were driven by water-power at a heavy cost. As in all the rising English industries the overshot wheel was generally used rather than the much less expensive undershot wheel. To turn the former a stream had to be diverted from its course, and a dam built to store up the water against a drought.

Among other industries introduced into England during the last sixty years of the sixteenth century, sugar-refining, brassmaking by the process of cementation, and the manufacture of saltpetre, apparently required a rather less extensive outlay in buildings, furnaces, boilers, machinery, tools, and materials than was frequently needed in those we have been considering. But all three manufactures were carried on in small factories. Sugar makers had to invest scores and sometimes hundreds of pounds in lead pipes, cisterns, copper kettles, and iron rollers for grinding the cane. Brass makers had to provide expensive metal pots, in which the copper was mixed with prepared calamine, and one or more large ovens in which eight or more of the pots were placed for heating. The "saltpetre men" had a comparable investment to make, for the preparation of saltpetre involved the mixing of the ingredients in a number of large tubs, followed by two long boilings of the liquid in copper kettles, heated by a big furnace of brickwork.

The introduction of all these manufactures into England during the last sixty years of the sixteenth century opened an entirely fresh field for the growth of industrial capitalism. It is important to form a rough impression of the number of enterprises, and of the influence upon industrial organization in Great Britain, of the new manufactures. While all of them gained a firm foothold in England before the Civil War, they had an earlier history in Europe, and some of them were carried on much more extensively abroad than in England. This was the case with paper-making and sugar-refining. Although ten or more papermills are known to have been at work in England in the thirties of the seventeenth century, the great new demand for **paper,** brought about by the growing importance of the printing press, continued to be met by imports, especially from France. Most of the sugar consumed in Great Britain was brought in refined from the West Indies. The other manufactures with which we have been dealing had made more headway in capturing the domestic market. England was becoming much less dependent upon imports for its supplies of alum, copperas, brass, and copper than for its supplies of paper and sugar, and the output of saltpetre and gunpowder were perhaps more than sufficient to meet native demands. English-made cannon proved so excellent in quality and so cheap in price that, before the end of Elizabeth's reign, they were in demand all over the Continent. Yet in each of these manufactures, the market could be supplied by a rather small number of factories. There were probably not more than a dozen, or at the most a score of large alum houses in the reign of Charles I, and neither the brass and battery works nor the powder mills and cannon foundries could have been much more numerous. Sussex, perhaps the principal seat of the cannon manufacture, apparently had only four foundries for casting cannons in 1613. Wars were still won with what seems to us an infinitesimal expenditure of metal and gunpowder. Yet it is clear that the number of considerable establishments at work in all these new manufactures, taken together, had reached several scores before the Civil War. And the introduction of such establishments, with their elaborate water-driven machinery, their large furnaces and accessories, must have had an influence upon the growth of industrial capitalism in England beyond that which can be measured in terms of the output or the number of workpeople engaged in them. Mechanics and inventors could study the new machinery, furnaces, and boilers with a view to adapting them to suit other processes of manufacture. Landlords and merchants, with capital to invest in other industries, were stimulated by example to

set up works on a larger scale than they might otherwise have done.

2. THE PROGRESS OF ADVANCED TECHNICAL METHODS IN OLD INDUSTRIES

A far greater number of workpeople and a far larger amount of capital were drawn into large-scale enterprise by the extensive changes in old industries than by the introduction of these "new" manufactures. The very rapid growth of markets for coal and ore was making it imperative to adopt less primitive methods in mining and the production of metals. As a result of the application of improved technical methods known before the middle of the sixteenth century, at least on the Continent, but not extensively used, conditions in these industries were largely transformed during the century following the dissolution of the monasteries.

Before the sixteenth century, in Great Britain, the expensive adit or long tunnel for draining mines was rare, machinery driven by water or horse power for pumping out water or raising minerals was almost unknown. The problems of prospecting for coal and ore, of sinking through rocky strata, and of ventilating the pits to force out noxious gases, hardly tried the ingenuity of the miner, for the depths of the workings seldom exceeded a few fathoms. Except at silver mines, which were scarce in Great Britain, and at a few very large tin and coal mines, mining seldom required the investment of much capital. Ore and coal were normally dug by independent partnerships of working miners.

Between 1540 and 1640, when copper ore was first sought after with sufficient zest to make the rights of the landowner to property in the mineral an important subject of judicial controversy before the Court of Exchequer, and when the output of coal probably increased at least eightfold, and the output of iron and lead ore several times over, it became necessary to sink to depths of twenty, thirty, and even forty or fifty fathoms. In many parts of England, Scotland and Wales, the miners were threatened by water which drowned out the workings, and by gas explosions which killed scores. During the reign of Elizabeth and her two Stuart successors, money was poured out lavishly in the construction of hundreds of drainage engines driven by water and more often by horse power, at tin, copper, and lead mines, and, above all, at collieries. As the digging and lining of an adit often cost thousands of pounds, and as the expense of operating a horse-driven pump sometimes amounted to about £2,000 a year, the new mining enterprises had to be conducted on a scale which would have seemed incredible to an Englishman of the time of Sir Thomas More. While the annual output of a coal mine before the middle of the sixteenth century had rarely exceeded a few hundred tons, and much of the mining had been done casually by manorial tenants, who worked part of the year as husbandmen, collieries producing 10,000 to 25,000 tons of coal, representing an investment of many thousands of pounds, and employing scores and sometimes hundreds of miners, became common before 1640 in the north of England, in Scotland, and even in the Midlands. By that time large enterprises were the rule in the mining of copper, as well as in the much less extensive mining of silver; they were common in the mining of tin and were not unknown in the mining of lead.

In the conversion of metallic ores into metals, and the preparation of these metals for the smiths, nailers, and other craftsmen who fashioned them into finished articles, large-scale enterprise made no less striking progress than in mining. The blast-furnace for producing cast-iron was probably introduced from the Continent towards the end of the fifteenth century. But it was little used in Sussex, the centre of the English iron industry, and apparently not at all elsewhere, until after 1540. Between 1540 and 1640, the process of iron-making assumed a new and highly capitalistic form, and the changes were second in importance

only to those which revolutionized the industry during and after the seventies of the eighteenth century. The ore came to be generally smelted in blast-furnaces, first in Sussex, then in Glamorganshire, Monmouthshire, the Midlands, the Forest of Dean, and Scotland. These furnaces were vast structures compared with the early forges. They often rose to a height of thirty feet and were usually more than twenty feet square at the bottom, with walls five or six feet thick of brick and stone to withstand the great heat necessary to obtain molten iron. The heat was generated with the help of a large leathern bellows about twenty feet long, usually driven by an overshot wheel almost as high as the furnace itself. To obtain the power, the water from a dam was carried high above the ground along a wooden trough, often 75 yards or more in length, to a point above the wheel. These new iron works involved an original outlay which normally exceeded a thousand pounds; they often employed scores of workmen to bring the materials, to convert wood to charcoal, to operate the machinery, and to handle the cast iron, and they were capable of producing from 100 to 500 tons or even more in a year. They were sometimes combined with, sometimes separate from, the finery and chafery, at which cast iron was made into wrought iron. The latter process was, in any case, scarcely less capitalistic than the former, for before the Civil War waterpower came to be generally employed both to fan the flames at the hearths and to drive the great hammers which forged the metal into bars. As early as 1607, Camden had commented upon the sound of the water-driven hammers throughout Sussex, which filled "the neighbourhood . . . night and day with continual noise." Whether the forges were situated near the furnace or at a distance they were often owned by the same entrepreneur or partnership, so that many ironmasters in calculating their outlay had to add the cost of the forge to that of the furnace.

Other branches of the metallurgical

industry were changing their form under the stimulus of technical improvements introduced from abroad. With the help of skilled workmen from Germany, copper smelting was combined with copper-mining in the gigantic financial enterprise of the Society of Mines Royal. Other metals were usually produced in less elaborate plants than iron and copper, and sometimes without the aid of machinery. But mills driven by water-power came to be extensively used in the last half of the sixteenth century for breaking lead ore, and for smelting and stamping tin. As a result, the process of smelting tin ores passed from the hands of small craftsmen to those of capitalist employers.

These changes of industrial organization in connection with the conversion of ores into metals were accompanied by similar changes in all the processes which supplied the craftsmen with standardized metal goods, in the form of ingots, sheets, rods, and wire. Steel had been made in England in small quantities throughout the Middle Ages, but the country had been mainly dependent for its supplies upon Germany. The first attempt to introduce a manufacture on a large scale occurred early in Elizabeth's reign in Sussex, Kent, and Glamorganshire, with the help of skilled Dutch technicians. Thirty foreign workmen were employed at a steel-work at Robertsbridge in Sussex, started in 1565, and the buildings included two large coal houses and a dwelling house, besides the work house and several forges. In James I's reign, cutting mills were set up in or near London for producing iron rods to be used by nailers, smiths, and shipwrights. The drawing of metal wire, which had been carried on exclusively by hand labour until the sixties of the sixteenth century, changed its character during the next few decades. Water-driven machinery was adopted both for hammering the metal bars into the proper form and for the actual drawing of the wire from the metal.

Large-scale industry was thus becoming the normal form of enterprise both in mining and in metallurgy. The adoption of new machinery and large furnaces was accompanied, as we saw, by a phenomenal expansion in the output of coal, and in a somewhat less striking growth in the output of metal. The demand for work-people was increasing nearly as rapidly as the output; for while the introduction of machinery reduced somewhat the labour-costs of producing metal from the ore, the advantages provided by labour-saving devices in mining were offset by the increasing difficulties of extracting coal and ore from greater depths. During the century preceding the Civil War, a great many thousands of men and women, whose ancestors had laboured on the land or as small craftsmen in their own homes in medieval towns and villages, were drawn into large-scale enterprise in mining and converting ore into a form of metal suitable for craftsmen to fashion into anchors, tools, machine parts, wool combs and cards, axle-trees, bits and spurs, grates, nails, locks and keys, ploughshares, kettles, pots and pans, and hundreds of other metal articles, which were wanted in much larger quantities than ever before as a result of the increase in population, the general expansion of industry, and the spread of comforts among the upper and middle classes.

While the progress of large-scale industry in mining and metallurgy from 1540 to 1640 was stimulated by the application of technical processes introduced with the help of skilled foreign artisans, it is probable that before the middle of the seventeenth century these processes were being more extensively used than in foreign nations. Great Britain was not only catching up with foreign countries; she had already begun to forge ahead of them. There was no growth in the output of coal abroad at all comparable to that in Great Britain, and, on the eve of the Civil War, three or four times as much coal was probably produced in Great Britain as in the whole of continental Europe. Britain had gained no comparable lead in the extraction of ores, but as coal mining already required the investment of more capital and the employment of more labour than all other kinds of British mining combined, it may be presumed that mining already occupied a more prominent place in the national economy than in any foreign country. Only the failure to solve the problem of smelting ore with coal had prevented Great Britain from capturing a place of equal pre-eminence in metallurgy.

With the critical shortage of timber that accompanied the industrial expansion of the Elizabethan Age, manufacturers spendthrift of fuel were heavily handicapped unless they could substitute coal, which was abundant and cheap, for firewood and charcoal, which were increasingly scarce and dear. Nowhere were the effects of rising timber prices felt more keenly than in smelting. The high cost of fuel began to check the expansion in the output of iron before the end of Elizabeth's reign; it brought the expansion to a standstill before the Civil War, and had begun to interfere with the production of lead, copper, and tin, all of which could be smelted with less fuel than iron. But the effects of the failure to solve the technical problem of substituting coal for wood in the process of converting ore to metal were somewhat less serious for the metallurgical industry as a whole than has sometimes been assumed. During the reigns of Elizabeth, James I, and Charles I, coal was successfully substituted for wood fuel in calcining the ores prior to their smelting, in remelting lead after it had been smelted, in extracting silver from lead, in converting iron into steel, in battery and wire work, and in nearly all the finishing processes. While Great Britain stood at a disadvantage in smelting as compared with continental countries, where the timber shortage became critical somewhat later, she had already obtained an advantage in the other metallurgical processes through the greater abundance and availability of her coal supplies. She had begun to supplement her domestic stock of metals by more substantial imports of iron from Flanders and Scandinavia.

3. THE DISCOVERY AND APPLICATION OF NEW TECHNICAL METHODS

The newly awakened interest in mechanical improvements, which spread among all classes in England from the nobility to the humblest artisan, and sent those who could afford it travelling in foreign countries for instruction, was not limited to the problem of saving firewood. In an age that Jevons and other nineteenth-century writers believed to be virtually barren of practical inventive achievement, England was actually becoming a busy hive of experiments designed to reduce labour. Shortly before the end of Elizabeth's reign, boring rods, for finding out the nature of underground strata, and railed ways with large horsedrawn waggons for carrying coal, were devised by the ingenuity of some inventors who remain anonymous, apparently in southern Nottinghamshire, where at about the same time, in 1589, William Lee gave the world his celebrated stocking-knitting frame.

It is impossible to determine to what extent workmen were drawn into largescale industry before 1640 as a result of English inventions. In some cases, the technical discoveries had little, if any, effects upon the form of industrial enterprise. Framework knitting remained a domestic manufacture until the nineteenth century, for Lee's invention did not cause a sufficiently great increase in the capital needed to draw it into the factory. Boring rods added something, but not much, to the costs of mining. Railed ways involved a far heavier outlay, especially where collieries were worked at some distance from navigable water, and where the terrain was full of hills and ravines. Their installation eliminated the independent local carter, who plied his horse and cart for hire, and changed the carriage of coal into a capitalistic industry. But neither railed ways nor boring rods made any great headway in connection with mining before the end of the seventeenth century.

The introduction of new furnaces, making possible the burning of coal, was of greater immediate importance. Calcining kilns added to the cost of iron works. Glass-making had been done by the foreign artisans, who introduced extensive commercial glass work into England after the middle of the sixteenth century, in specially built houses, with oblong furnaces about six feet long, before the invention of closed pots; so it would be inaccurate to say that the invention converted a domestic into a factory industry. But it furthered the concentration of capital, and had far-reaching consequences for the progress of British glass manufacture. It was not only that the new houses for producing sheet glass were larger structures, costing more to build and equip and employing more hands than those for producing fine goblets and mirrors which they partly superseded; the labour done at the new houses was of a different nature. Glass-making as carried on at Altare and Venice in the late fifteenth and sixteenth centuries, and as taught by the Italians to the French, the Dutch, and the English, was an art, and the persons who practised it in Italy enjoyed a prestige and dignity similar to that attaching to a goldsmith, or even a sculptor and painter. An Italian glass goblet of the early sixteenth century can be appropriately set beside Benvenuto Cellini's saltcellar or a fine canvas by Carpaccio. But the new glass furnaces in seventeenth-century England came to be staffed largely with stokers and other unskilled workers, whose social status resembled that of workers in alum houses. It was the coarsest glass — especially such as was used for windows and bottles — which consumed the greatest quantities of coal, and was made in the biggest houses; and the English especially excelled in the manufacture of this cheap glass, wanted much more generally now that the use of glass windows and vessels was becoming common, and that luxuries were spreading from the highest to the middle orders.

4. OTHER FACTORS CAUSING THE CONCENTRATION OF INDUSTRIAL CAPITAL

The adoption of mechanical methods,

little used in Great Britain before the Reformation or discovered during the following century, clearly played an important role in the rapid growth of large-scale industry between 1540 and 1640. But there were manufactures in which the factory form of enterprise made remarkable headway without any fundamental change in the technique of production. Two principal factors were making large-scale industry more economical, even without the introduction of labour-saving machinery or new types of furnace. One was the growth in the size of the markets; the other was the shift from wood to coal fuel in a great many branches of industry, where the substitution involved no technical problem.

In no industry perhaps was the increase in the scale of manufacture more impressive than in the making of salt by the evaporation of sea-water. The growth of population in London and other towns caused a great increase in the demand for salt to be used in preserving fish and meat; and the advantages offered by abundant supplies of an inferior grade of coal, which would have gone to waste at the mine but for the saltworks, drew the growing industry to the colliery districts. During the last two decades of the sixteenth century and the first three of the seventeenth, most of the sea-salt manufacture in Great Britain came to be concentrated at the mouth of the Tyne and Wear and along the coasts of the Firth of Forth. The old casual workings of local peasants were superseded by great iron pans twenty feet and more square, and five or six feet deep, in which sea-water was evaporated by the heat of a great furnace. The whole structure was set in a wooden house, which also served as a storing place for the supplies of coal and often as a dwelling place for the workmen recruited into this labour. Many scores of pounds were required to set up such a plant, and although only four workmen were needed to keep a single pan in operation, the principal salt works were composed of many such pans, clustered together. As early as 1589, one capitalist claimed to employ 300 men at salt works on the Wear in which he had invested £4,000. The works at South Shields, which came into the hands of the State at the time of the Civil War, employed about 1,000 men, and represented an original investment of many thousands of pounds.

Changes in the supplies of fuel and raw materials and a growth in the markets for the products also combined to bring about a similar increase in the scale of enterprise in soap-boiling, and a slower increase in the scale of enterprise in lime-burning and brewing.

5. CONCLUSION

It must not be supposed that the developments we have attempted to sketch came to an end at the time of the Civil War. While work-people were probably drawn into large-scale industry at a somewhat less rapid rate in the century following than in the century preceding 1640, the striking changes in technique and the striking concentration of capital which began in the Elizabethan Age led directly to the rapid industrial progress of the late eighteenth and nineteenth centuries. The rise of industrialism can be more properly regarded as a long process stretching back to the middle of the sixteenth century and coming down to the final triumph of the industrial state towards the end of the nineteenth, than as a sudden phenomenon associated with the late eighteenth and early nineteenth centuries. It is no longer possible to find a full explanation of "the great inventions" and the new factories of the late eighteenth century in a preceding commercial revolution which increased the size of markets.

The commercial revolution, if that is the proper term to apply to a rapid growth in foreign and domestic trade during a period of two centuries, had a continuous influence reaching back to the Reformation upon industrial technology and the scale of mining and manufacturing. But so, in turn, the progress of industry had continually stimulated in a variety of ways the progress of commerce. The former progress was quite as "revolutionary" as the latter, and quite as directly responsible for the "Industrial Revolution."

Before the dissolution of the monasteries, Great Britain was, industrially, in a backwater compared with Italy, Spain, the Low Countries, the South-German states, and even France. Englishmen had almost nothing to teach foreigners in the way of practical mechanical knowledge, except in connection with the production of tin and the manufacture of pewter. By the end of the century, the position was reversed.

It was probably not, as has been supposed, during the late eighteenth and early nineteenth centuries that the contrast between industrial progress in England and in continental countries was most striking, but in the two centuries preceding the "Industrial Revolution." As the continuous rapid progress of industrial capitalism appears to cover the longest period of time in England, the concept of an "Industrial Revolution" would seem to be especially inappropriate as an explanation of the triumph of industrial civilization in Great Britain. It gives the impression that the process was especially sudden, when in all probability it was more continuous than in any other country.

THE "REVOLUTION" NOT COMPLETE BY 1851

JOHN H. CLAPHAM

With the exception of a few early years teaching Economics at Leeds, Clapham spent all his working life at Cambridge. He was Professor of Economic History and Vice-Provost of King's College, and he continued to teach during World War II (after his formal retirement) and until his death in 1946. His principal interests lay in eighteenth century France (he wrote a biography of the Abbé Siéyès) and nineteenth century Britain. The excerpt which follows is from his greatest book, and consists of the material on the principal textile industries, which have always been taken as the most rapidly "revolutionized," but which Clapham shows to have been incompletely transformed in the 1830's, and even in 1851. By temperament, one feels, as well as by the pressure of the evidence on a scholarly mind, Clapham rejected the sensational, the catastrophic, in history, and stressed variety and slowness of growth.

I

BECAUSE no single British industry had passed through a complete technical revolution before 1830, the country abounded in ancient types of industrial organization and in transitional types of every variety. Even in cotton spinning the early wooden machinery with metal fittings was in common use; the "self-acting" mule, built of metal, was but newly invented and only used in the more progressive mills. There were still plenty of wooden spinning jennies, turned by hand, in the Lancashire mills in 1824, though the drawing process, preparatory to spinning, was always done by power. But nine years later "those that are now jenny-spinners are getting, I think, into the decline of life," so quickly was the industry moving. Weaving by the new method was just entering on the stage of rapid development, after twenty years of experiment

and hostility. The first Manchester steam-loom factory had been set up in 1806. Guest's estimate for 1818 was that fourteen such factories existed in Manchester, Salford, Middleton, Hyde, Stayley Bridge and elsewhere: he thought they contained about 2,000 looms. Writing in 1823 he reckoned that "at present not less than 10,000" power looms were at work in Great Britain. They made chiefly common print cloth and shirtings, but were rapidly conquering new lines of work. He supposed that there were 360,000 cotton weavers in the country, but probably his guess was high. An estimate made in 1830 put the figures for England and Scotland at 55,000–60,000 power looms and 240,000 hand looms. Baines, writing in 1835, did not anticipate the rapid disappearance of the older instrument, and his anticipation proved right.

The wool industries, because of their

From John H. Clapham, *An Economic History of Modern Britain*, (London, 1930, 1932), Volume I, Second Edition, Chapter 5, pp. 143–5, 147–8, 157–8, 159–62, 178–81, 184–5, 192–3; Volume II, Chapter 2, pp. 26–32. By permission of Cambridge University Press.

antiquity, their long regulation by the state — which cotton had entirely escaped — their wide distribution, and the extreme complexity of their products, had as yet been very incompletely transformed. Even the flying-shuttle was not in "very general use" in the West Riding until round about 1800. Carpet weavers still threw the shuttle across the loom by hand in the old ancient way, down to 1840 and later. The worsted, that is to say, the combed wool, yarn was now almost entirely mill spun on the frame, though even the distaff was not quite extinct in England in 1820; but the essential preliminary process of combing was a handicraft in spite of various experiments in machine combing. There was an analogous gap in the process of wool spinning. Here the preliminary business of carding had been among the first to be taken over by power in the chief manufacturing areas, carding "engines" — cylinders set with wire teeth and revolving against one another to open out the wool — being often installed in the old water-driven fulling mills. But, in between carding and spinning there came, in 1835, when Ure published his *Philosophy of Manufacture*, what he called a "handicraft operation," that of "slubbing" or preparing the rough rope of wool, which was to be spun on the mule, on a wooden, hand-worked, machine called a "billy." "The slubbers," Ure writes, "though inmates of factories, are not, properly speaking, factory workers, being independent of the moving power." He noted that a patent had just been announced in December 1834, by which a second carding engine could prepare and deliver, by the process now known as condensing, the loose rope for the mule. The general adoption of this critical invention only took place in the second half of the century.

In a backward district such as Gloucestershire, even the mule only began to come into use about 1828, the hand-worked "billy" leading to the spinning "jenny," also worked by hand; though carding and some other processes were done by power.

Of the weaving of wool and other textiles, it need only be said here that power was first tried experimentally, with the usual result — a riot, for the relatively light fabrics of the worsted industry in the early 'twenties, and that power weaving remained experimental down to 1830. For the heavier woollen broad-cloths, pilot-cloths, uniform-cloths, blankets and the like, the power-loom had not yet been tried. Nor had it, as may be supposed, in carpet-weaving, and only tentatively in the roughest linen-weaving and for some kinds of silks. A committee reporting in 1830 discussed, as a speculative question, what might happen "should it ever be found practicable to make use of it extensively in the fabric of woollens or silks." Next year Lardner expressed himself as "very doubtful whether" its use was "susceptible of much extension in any save the commonest branches of the silk manufacture."

Machinery had already gripped a number of the final textile processes. The grip was not always a new thing. For centuries, in the "fulling stocks," the big water-driven hammers had thudded down on the wet cloth, beating and thickening it; though in eighteenth-century London the motive power was a horse. Shearing the nap of the cloth mechanically instead of with monstrous scissors, had prevailed against the bitter opposition of the shearmen, and was in general use. So was the printing of calico by rollers, an invention comparatively recent but quickly adopted because the rollers were easily driven even by ordinary "milling" machinery. Metal rolling by water power was an old story and the mere mechanism was similar. It was easy also to use power to drive the heavy "calendars or mangles" used to glaze cloth, silk, linen and calico. Pressing and packing by hydraulic power followed rather rapidly on Bramah's invention of the hydraulic press in 1795; for they had penetrated to Dundee by the 'twenties. The revolution in dyeing, by chemistry not by the machine, was as yet far in the future; but Berthollet's chemical knowledge had begun to revolutionize bleaching and help make a new industry.

The old Scottish adjunct to the power of sun and rain for bleaching had been sour milk. This had been to some extent replaced, after 1764, by very dilute sulphuric acid. Twenty-one years later came Berthollet's suggested use of chlorine-water, which he had expounded to James Watt in 1786. Next year de Saussure — it is a string of great names — showed it to Professor Copeland of Aberdeen, whose business friends tried it at once. By the early years of the nineteenth century, the commercial preparation of chlorine had been much improved by Charles Tennant of Glasgow. His works at St. Rollox were started about the year 1800. By 1830 they covered ten acres of ground. The main products were sulphuric acid, chloride of lime, soda and soap. Lancashire was rather later than Glasgow in producing chemicals on a large scale. The first important works for the manufacture of soda by the Leblanc process were started by Muspratt at Liverpool in 1823 — the year in which Huskisson cut the excise duty on salt, the raw material, from 15s. to 2s. a bushel. Six years later, salt being now quite free of duty, after "bitter opposition from agricultural interests," Muspratt and a partner started manufacturing in the pleasant little country town which had grown up during the eighteenth century about St. Helen's chapel, in the parish of Prescot. Meanwhile Leblanc's process had taken root on the north-east coast in the old seaside salt industry. Experiments with it had been made so early as 1806 by William Losh who had worked under Lavoisier, backed by the Earl of Dundonald; but the serious start was made by the Cooksons at Gateshead and Losh at Walker during the 'twenties, in connection with the repeal of the excise duty.

When the new power and the new machines, with their almost unlimited transforming capacity, were let loose on Britain, towards the end of the eighteenth century, they struck a society in which — although the old powers of water and wind were very extensively used, implements of many kinds were long familiar, and capitalism with or without machinery and power was well established — the most primitive forms of industrial organization still survived, not merely as fossils or as curiosities. The Highlands were not representative; but it is worth recalling that the Highlander at the very end of the eighteenth century still "made his own shoes of his own tanning. . . . Every man there is Jack of all Trades." The women extracted dyes from herbs, trees and shrubs of their own growing. The spinning-wheel was just coming in; teams of women, who sang as they worked, did the fulling by hand. The cloth "will take another song," they would say. But even the Highland women did not "in general now work at the loom as they formerly did," the loom of 1797 being less suited for women than the primitive "beart" which had been in general use a generation or so earlier. In the Lowlands and Northern England this direct production by the household for its own use did not go so far, but it was still important in the 'nineties of the eighteenth century. Of "the Midland and Southern counties," however, it could already be said that "the labourer, in general, purchases a very considerable proportion, if not the whole of his cloaths, from the shopkeepers." Eden had countryfolk, including country manufacturers, in mind; and primarily small farmers, yeomen, and such. He allowed that some labourers were too poor to buy raw material, but omitted to explain how they got clothing; and parts of his account are obviously inapplicable to townsmen. But real townsmen were still a small minority in the North in 1797. The classes of whom he wrote retained at least some of these habits thirty years later, in spite of the growth of pride and broad-cloth.

When the Highland women abandoned the "beart" they had handed over weaving to a representative of that grade which, in the logical classification of methods of industrial organization, comes next above household production proper, in which producer and consumer are one — to the household weaver as he was called in medieval England, the "customer weaver" of early nineteenth-century descriptions, who worked up the consumer's prepared material to the consumer's order. Throughout Scotland and parts of Wales in 1825–30 this was the normal arrangement in rural districts; it was still to be found in Northern England, though mainly for linen weaving alone, and it was not yet quite extinct south of the Trent. It has been said that "in the Midlands at the end of the eighteenth century 'in every parish there was a weaver; and he was never called by his own name, but *the weaver.*'" The reminiscences here quoted come from Nottinghamshire and it is doubtful whether, even at the date referred to, any such general survival could be demonstrated for the southern Midlands; though certainly customer weavers were known there. Nottingham and Lincoln, as it happens, were the most southerly counties in which a fair number of them survived forty years later (1835–40). "These domestic artisans were at one time numerous in the counties of Lincoln and Nottingham. Their number is now much reduced." That, too, is the country of their nineteenth-century representative in literature, Silas Marner.

They were reported from every Scottish shire by the careful schoolmaster officials of the 1831 Census, mixed up in the industrial counties, and in some others, with market weavers — outworkers for urban employers — but completely unadulterated in the far North. In the county of Inverness, for instance, there was a customer weaver for every 279 of the population. At the other end of the country, in Berwickshire, if the figures could be trusted, there would seem to have been one for every 100; but as, besides the customer weavers, there were reported weavers "distinctly said to be employed by the Master Manufacturers of Edinburgh and Glasgow," probably some not so reported were also employed. Behind the bald figures and brief notes of the Census can be seen going forward in Scotland a process which in England had begun certainly in the thirteenth century, and perhaps earlier, the transformation of

these household weavers into piece-workers not for the consumer, but for the organizer of production in a town. Customer weavers in Scotland, during the decade 1820–30, still handled both linen and woollen yarns; but the transformation of the wool industry was tending to restrict that side of their work in the South. There, as in England, the customer weaver put up his last fight on a field of sheets and table-linen.

In Wales there were numbers of weavers working up home-spun woollen yarn in every county in 1831. But in many cases weaving for the customer's use was not their sole, or main, business; for throughout North Wales there was a well-organized production of flannels for market, which in the county of Montgomery — at Newton and Llanidloes in particular — was passing into the factory stage. Even farm-produced flannel went to market and it was hard to differentiate a weaver from a farm hand. "The farmers make their pieces in their own houses from their own wool," a Montgomeryshire witness explained seven years later, "and they bring them to Newtown market. . . . Agricultural labourers about Llanbrynmair are hired by the year; they can all weave or spin; the farmers employ them at out-door work in the summer, and at the loom or jenny in the winter." It will be noted that the jenny had beaten the wheel. But the true customer weaver was common even in 1838 in South Wales, and the account given of him then had been applicable to more individuals and over a wider area ten or fifteen years earlier. "Thirty or forty years ago" [say 1800–1810] the "isolated parish weaver" "occupied a very prominent station in the country, ranking in point of number and importance with the blacksmith and the miller; there being generally one or more in every parish, with fulling-mills in proportion." "In the retired parts of the country this description of person might still be found [in 1838], in the proportion of perhaps one in every two or three parishes, or even more." The hand-spun and parish-woven cloth was reckoned three times as durable as "shop-cloth." The looms were heavy and "mostly very old, as new looms would scarcely answer the cost of making. Many of them are perhaps some centuries old." Even in South Wales, it should be added, tiny "woollen factories" with a staff of from five to ten, equipped with carding-sets, hand or water driven, hand-worked jennies and handlooms, were thinly scattered over the country by 1838. It was their gradual appearance which had so much lowered the status of the parish weaver during the previous generation.

For the North of England, it is difficult to disentangle the surviving customer weavers from the market weavers; obviously so in Lancashire, Cheshire, the West Riding and Cumberland — which had an important textile centre at Carlisle — and Westmorland, which was dominated from Kendal. Of Northumberland the 1831 Census states that: "the woollen-yarn and linen-thread, still spun in the villages, employs about 300 weavers, scattered thro'out the County." The North Riding was full of scattered linen weavers, but they were within reach of the market influences of Knaresborough and Leeds, and some were certainly market weavers congregated in the smaller towns. The customer weavers of Lincolnshire are referred to in the Census notes, as they are in the Hand Loom Weavers Report seven or eight years later, where the reference shows that they had mainly been working at linen. It can serve as their epitaph. "Their number is now much reduced, there being far less domestic manufacture [of yarn]. The cheapness of cotton goods is considered the principal cause. Some . . . employ themselves partly in agriculture. . . . In a commercial point of view these men are totally insignificant, and can excite no interest but as a remnant of a body once very numerous in the generations now gone past." From the scanty and incomplete figures available it may be estimated that, for the whole of Great Britain, they numbered not less than 5,000 and not more than 10,000 in 1831.

When a medieval gild forbade journeymen to take work home or to work for more than one master, the policy, there can be little doubt, was intended to prevent them from becoming mere outworkers, not so much in their own interests — journeymen did not make the rules — as because, once outwork is well established, the master with most character and commercial skill outstrips his fellows, drawing into his service a disproportionate share of the available labour. The gilds believed in equality of opportunity for masters. In the long run the gilds failed; and outwork became the predominant — though never the sole — form of capitalistic industrial organization in Britain. Probably it was still the predominant form in the reign of George IV; for though it was losing ground on one side to great works and factories, it was always gaining on the other at the expense of household production and handicraft. Capitalistic outwork may be said to be fully established only when the material belongs to the trading employer, and is returned to him after the process for which the outworker's skill is required has been completed — the wool given out to be spun, the yarn given out to be woven, the shirt given out for "seam and gusset and band," the nail-rod to be returned as nails, the limbs to be returned as dolls, the leather coming back as boots.

Among British outworkers the hand-loom weavers occupied the most prominent place. Hand-spinning for an employer, whether on the distaff or the wheel, was all but dead in England — a generation and a half, at most, of mill-spinning had killed it — and was already decadent in Scotland and Wales. Apart from perhaps 20,000 to 30,000 cotton power-looms, and a few experimental power-looms in linen and worsted and silk weaving, every loom in Britain was hand worked in the late 'twenties. No census of them was ever taken: but there cannot have been fewer than 500,000 and there may have been very many more. The vast majority of the weaving families were employers' outworkers. There were the 5,000 to 10,000 customer weavers. There were also a certain number of journeymen weavers, who worked looms belonging to small masters on the master's premises, and of factory or shop weavers employed in the loom-shops of large manufacturers; but even in 1841 it could be stated that "neither the factory weavers nor the journeymen form large portions of the weaving population." Normally, the weaver owned his loom or looms — so much fixed capital at least was his — but sometimes he hired it, or hired some of the "tackle" for it. The latter arrangement was common in figured weaving, particularly the weaving of figured silks. Where the employer was loom-owner or tackle-owner his hold on the workman was strengthened; but it was already strong enough, by 1825–30, owing to the growing competition among weavers, especially in the plain cotton trade, as the Irish crowded into Lancashire and the West of Scotland and the power-loom began to tell. Not every hand-loom weaver was a mere employer's outworker. In the North some had a foot on the land; but this did not help the cotton weaver much as competition grew more bitter.

Textile workers other than weavers were, by this time, mostly to be found on the employer's premises — in factory or shop. In wool-combing, however, the situation was complex. The comber might be a pure domestic outworker, combing by the piece for a worsted-spinner or wool-stapler, that is to say, wool grader and merchant. But he might also be a journeyman engaged in the "comb-shop" of a small master, an arrangement common in combing though rare in weaving. Small master-combers had been a recognized industrial type in the eighteenth century — before the days of spinning machinery — and, until combing machinery became generally effective, they survived. Work done for them was outwork from the spinner's, but not from the master-comber's, point of view. The need for combing to be done on the employer's premises had been increased because, right down to the end of the eighteenth century, a large body of itinerant unmarried combers followed the wool-clips, as Irishmen followed harvest, and combed for local sta-

plers. This class was declining with the concentration of the worsted industry and the death of cottage spinning — for in the old days wool could be both combed and spun conveniently near its place of growth — but it was not yet extinct. Lastly, some of the worsted-spinning mills collected hand combers on the premises, factory workers detached from the power.

When factory legislation began, cotton-spinners constantly protested against the singling out of their industry for control and the censure which control implies. Their arguments were often sound; but the action of the reformers and of parliament is easily comprehensible. Long hours and overworked children were certainly not confined to cotton-spinning; but there was a wholesaleness, a monstrosity, about the great cotton mills which marked them down for public notice; although the less observant and less sensitive public of the eighteenth century had paid little attention to the perhaps greater evils of silk-throwing mills, some few of which were almost equally monstrous. Small concerns there were of course in quantity, in the early days of cotton-spinning machinery, and in them some of the worst abuses. Dan Kenworthy told a committee in 1832 how when he was a lad they constantly worked "day and night the back end of the week and all Sunday." "Who?" said the committee. "Only my sister and her husband and me; sometimes another boy." "Do you mean . . . these were all the work-people employed?" "Yes; belonging to that business." But the size of the average steam spinning mill in the chief manufacturing centres, even in 1815–16, was something unprecedented in British industry. Forty-one Glasgow mills averaged 244 workpeople each. Three mills in the neighboring country, all owned by one firm — Jas. Finlay and Co. — averaged over 500; and, at New Lanark, Dale and Owen employed over 1,600. In England, the Strutts, at Belper and Millford, had 1,494 workpeople. A list of forty-three important mills, in and about Manchester, gave an average employment figure of exactly 300:

two firms out of the forty-three, McConnel and Kennedy, and George and Adam Murray, each employed more than 1,000. In the year of the Reform Bill, a similar list of about the same number of Manchester mills gives a figure of nearly 401.

When the spinner also controlled the organization of weaving, an arrangement rare in 1816 but become common before 1830, the aggregate figures of mill workers and outworking weavers were, in extreme cases, gigantic. Monteith, Bogle and Co., of Glasgow, in 1816, had 4,000 workers on their books — spinners, some power-loom weavers, 300 dyers in two distinct dyeworks, and an army of outworking muslin weavers. At the same date Horrocks, Miller and Co., of Preston, employed 700 spinners, in four separate mills, and a whole countryside of hand-loom weavers, nearly 7,000 people all told.

These are all the great concerns. Average figures would be immensely reduced were it possible to include the mills of the type in which Dan Kenworthy worked down to 1814. But when, in the course of the next twenty years, the smallest type had been almost squeezed out and the combination of spinning and power-loom weaving had become rather more common, the average cotton mill visited by the newly appointed inspectors, in the early 'thirties, employed on the premises certainly under 200, but probably upwards of 150, people.

In partially revolutionized industries the large power-using unit was becoming common, but was not yet really representative. This is true of the textile industries, other than cotton. There were, of course, large businesses and large wool, linen, and silk mills. English flax and worsted spinning were following in the tracks of the cotton industry. Marshall's flax mills at Leeds were quite comparable with the larger Manchester factories — and more unhealthy than any of them. There were already some big worsted spinning mills in the Bradford district. But weaving, both woollen and worsted, was still normally done "out," though some employers had gathered all

their workpeople under their own eye, like Wormald Gott and Wormalds of Leeds, in whose mill — rebuilt after a fire in 1799 — "the whole process of manufacture . . . from the first breaking of the wool to the finishing of the piece . . . was conducted on a very extensive scale." It is easy to exaggerate, in imagination, the size of the mills; and there are no general figures from the 'twenties with which to check the imagination. But from the 'thirties there are. Andrew Ure calculated in 1835, from the returns of the first factory inspectors, that the average woollen or worsted mill contained 44.6 persons, mainly women and children. A rather later and more exact calculation, based on material collected in 1839, gives a corresponding figure of 58, and shows that the average employment figure in 342 Yorkshire worsted mills, the giant concerns of the wool industries, was just over 75. That is after ten or fifteen years of rapid growth both of the industries and of their constituent units. Mills were being built very fast in the early 'thirties; "enough to astonish anybody," said a witness in 1833. If figures existed for 1825–30, thirty-five to forty employees for factories in the wool industries taken *en bloc*, and fifty to sixty for worsted spinning, might not be unreasonable. Factory *plus* outwork figures for the larger firms would be much greater; for in many cases, particularly in the woollen industry in its then stage of development, a minority of work was done on the premises. In worsted a man might be a spinner and nothing else, but in the larger woollen firms the control of production from start to finish was in the same hands — whether the work was done "in" or "out." A maker of army broadcloth from Wakefield told the committee on the combination laws in 1825 that he employed over four hundred people, including his weavers, and a Huddersfield witness, speaking of one of the great men of his district in the fancy woollen trade, said: "we consider them considerable men when they have a hundred weavers, but he has nearly three hundred." Eight years later, John Brooke of Huddersfield "supposed he employed" upwards of a thousand in- and out-workers, and "one of the largest superfine manufactories in the whole of the West of England" claimed fifteen hundred.

On the other side of the account, whether the average business or the average factory is being measured, must be set the big battalions of the Yorkshire domestic clothiers. In the first decade of the century it was reckoned that more than 3,000 of them came in to sell their pieces in the two chief cloth halls of Leeds; and there were other important selling halls in the West Riding, besides another small one in Leeds itself. Their numbers had decreased by 1820; but even twenty-five years later Leon Faucher was greatly impressed by their sustained strength: "c'est en Angleterre qu'il faut aller pour voir, tant que l'humble édifice subsiste encore, cette exception toute démocratique aux progrès absorbants de la grande industrie." The edifice still had considerable resisting power; for in 1858 the historian of Yorkshire explained that only about half those engaged in the woollen industry worked in factories — outside were a great majority of piece-working weavers and a minority of the still independent domestic clothiers.

II

Nothing is more remarkable than the complete localization [by 1851] of some textile industries and the attainment by others of a localization which, although not complete, was not to be altered appreciably during the next half-century. Under pressure of bad times in the 'forties, cotton had fallen back on South Lancashire and the adjacent parts of Cheshire and the West Riding, leaving a strong detached force in Clydesdale and various weak ones in other districts. From nearly a dozen English and Scottish counties came complaints of local falls in population resulting from the closing down of cotton mills. The area with the better competitive facilities had come best through a spell of bad trade. Of approximately 527,000 cotton workers in the country, some 312,000 were in Lancashire, 55,000 in Cheshire and the West Riding, and 58,000 in Lanarkshire.

The most complete concentration was that of the worsted industry into the West Riding. Its oldest home, Norwich, had been losing ground ever since the eighteenth century, but was still a fairly active manufacturing centre in 1831, though it had adopted little modern machinery, if any. By 1841 the trade was nearly dead: during that decade the population of Norwich had stood still. About 1840 a belated attempt to recover the old industry was made by the establishment of spinning mills. Norwich had been buying yarn from Yorkshire and she wished to end this dependence. It was much too late; for in the next few years Yorkshire perfected combing machinery and went ahead again. In 1850 the factory inspectors reported nearly 865,000 worsted spindles and 32,617 power-looms for worsted in England: there were hardly any in Scotland or Wales. Of the spindles 746,000 and of the looms 30,850, were in Yorkshire. Norfolk had 19,216 spindles and 428 looms. The thing was done, a clean decisive defeat. Worsted had become the Yorkshire industry which it would remain.

The woollen manufacture had almost reached the pitch of concentration which it showed in the twentieth century. It was, and is, less concentrated than cotton and much less concentrated than worsted. Of 138,000 people who described themselves as engaged in it in 1851 only 56,000 were in the West Riding; 15,000 in Scotland; 11,000 in Lancashire; 9,000 in Gloucestershire; 7,000 in Wiltshire — and the rest scattered over the remaining counties of England and Wales as the industries map suggests, Devon being the county next to Wiltshire in order of importance. Fifty years later the West Riding had still only half the woollen spindles in the kingdom, which implies only a slight increase of concentration during that long and economically decisive age.

Just as cotton had drawn into Lancashire

and wool into the West Riding, so flax was drawing northward into Scotland — and out of Great Britain altogether into Ulster. It had already ceased to be a really important English industry; for of some 103,000 people engaged in it in Britain no less than 77,000 were Scots, largely hand-loom weavers.

Silk still held out against the mechanical and geographical forces which were making for concentration. There were indeed more silk workers in mechanical Lancashire than in any other county, whereas Lancashire had hardly been reckoned a silk county at all thirty years earlier. In Cheshire the old nucleus of workers had grown with the aid of machinery to 22,000. But there were many about Coventry, where power was little used: there were still 16,000 in London and from 2,000 to 6,000 in each of six other counties. In nearly every place where there was any textile manufacturing, some silk was worked and the industry persisted in a few places where there was no other.

It is not easy to exaggerate the importance of the textile manufactures in the industrial life of the country. Although not even that of cotton was completely mechanized — there may have been still 40,000 to 50,000 cotton hand-looms at work — they stood as the representative industries of the age of machinery and power, even though coal-mining and metallurgy had more final significance. Because they were so much mechanized their output was prodigious. Because they were not completely mechanized they carried with them in their march, and often left to fall by the wayside, a host of those who had now become hand-working camp-followers. Not counting hosiery and lace, they found employment for — or should we say gave a trade name to? — nearly eleven hundred thousand people.

Their social importance can perhaps be best brought out by a comparison of 1851 with 1901. The comparison is not statistically exact at all points, but is quite exact enough for purposes of illustration:

	1851	1901
Population of Great Britain	20,960,000	37,000,000
Cotton workers (in 1851 with printers, dyers, etc.)	527,000	544,000
Wool workers	284,000	235,000
Silk workers	133,000	37,000
Linen and hemp workers (in 1901 with jute)	134,000	99,000
Textile printers, dyers, etc.		79,000
	1,078,000	994,000

That is to say, the trades, or their nearest equivalents, which at the opening of the twentieth century employed 1 in 37 of the population had employed 1 in 19 in the year of the Great Exhibition. The hand-working camp-followers outside the mills, and the relative imperfection of machinery inside, account for the astonishing figures of 1851. It is to be remembered that, although there were nearly 250,000 power-looms in the cotton industry in 1850, there were less than 33,000 in worsted, less than 10,000 in woollen, barely 6,000 in flax and not 1,200 in silk.

Even in spinning, mechanization was not complete, though true hand-spinning was dead in the factory districts, and nearly all the decisive inventions had been made. About 1830, American inventors had introduced the cap and the ring spindles, which were to become important in the worsted and cotton industries. But neither was economically decisive, for neither affected industrial organization or greatly extended the empire of the machine; they were just improvements on the flyer spindle which Arkwright had borrowed from the spinning wheel. Nor had either gained a secure footing in Britain by 1850, and thereafter their progress was slow. That of the British-invented self-acting mule had not been quick, nor was it to become so; a fact of special interest because only with the arrival of the self-actor did mule-spinning become completely automatic. In the old "hand mule," although power supplied the main motive force, the "carriage" on which the spindles are ranked was pulled out and pushed back by the spinner, the yarn being drawn out fine and twisted on the outward run and wound on to the bobbin on the return. It was the toil of this pushing and pulling that a deputation of cotton-spinners once illustrated to Lord Palmerston with a heavy arm-chair in his own drawing-room. The effective self-actor had been invented by Roberts of Manchester in 1825. By 1834 his firm had made 520 self-actors with over 200,000 spindles, and they were hoping to double the number in 1834–35. But like so many new machines, the self-actor was for a long time too rough for the finest work — it did not wind the yarn well on the bobbin, for one thing — and too dear for the smaller spinners. When the great New Lanark mills were sold, for the second or third time, in 1851, they contained 28,900 self-actor spindles, but also 13,600 "hand-mule spindles." "On account of the excessive cost very few firms were able to purchase the self-actor," a secretary of the Oldham Master Spinners wrote long after, "and therefore hand-mules were the rule and self-actor mules the exception." In the early 'fifties few self-actors were used in fine-spinning districts such as that of Bolton, and they were far from universal in the districts which span the medium and coarse counts.

In woollen spinning, as has already been noted, the operation of slubbing, which Andrew Ure had called a handicraft in 1834, had been little changed. The original "slubbing billy" was a hand-worked machine like the original jenny. Child piecers rubbed together gauzy strips of wool from the carding engine, to be roughly spun on the billy before going to their final spinning on the jenny or mule. By 1850 the billy might be power driven, but the arduous piecing work for it remained. Even eight years later Edward Baines of Leeds, when describing the local industry before the British Association, treated the billy as normal, though he spoke of a "new machine called the condenser" which would cut out billy and piecers and link the carding machine direct to the mule.

Precisely in the year 1851 a textile invention perhaps more decisive than that of the self-acting mule was completed for England: Donisthorpe and Lister perfected a wool-combing machine which became at once commercially successful. There had been combing machines since Cartwright's day, but his Big Ben, though it had alarmed the hand-combers, neither ruined them nor made a fortune for Cartwright. They could still do better work than any machine. Down to about 1840 their position was reasonably safe — safe from machinery if not from themselves; for their trade was easily learned and the immigrant Irish took to it, with other unskilled and half-skilled men. Then came the effective machines. All through the 'forties in England and France the inventors ultimately successful were at work — Donisthorpe, Heilmann, Lister, Holden, Noble. Heilmann succeeded first, and his patents were sold most profitably to English firms for use not only in the worsted but also in the cotton and flax industries. Lister and Donisthorpe adopted one of his central principles; and though Lister claimed that they had mastered all the difficulties connected with the invention "before M. Heilmann's patent was heard of," Heilmann's representatives secured a verdict for infringement against them in 1852. Next year the comb named after Noble — though it seems to have been mainly the work of Donisthorpe — came on the market; and a few years later Holden, a second collaborator with Lister, perfected another type of comb upon which he had first worked in 1847–48 or earlier.

These two men were not simple inventors; they were industrial organizers and combatants of the first rank, and Lister, a gentleman born, started with some capital. They had a European view. In conjunction they had started a combing mill at St. Denis in 1849. Within a few years Lister dominated the industry. He sold machines to spinners for a royalty of £1,000 each. By 1855 he had five English, three French and one German mill combing on commission for spinners. Never before had a factory industry been more quickly born, once the long gestation was over; nor did one ever grow more quickly. By 1857 James, the contemporary historian of the worsted industry, could write that "by far the larger proportion of the wool worked up in the worsted branch is combed by machinery," and could add that "far the greater proportion of all the wool . . . now combed is combed by Lister's machine." A single Lister comb would do the work of a hundred skilled men easily, and do it very much better. Thus wool-combing was mechanized.

THE ORIGIN OF THE
INDUSTRIAL CAPITALIST

KARL MARX

Born in Prussia, Marx spent most of his life as an exile, first in France, then, for more than thirty years before his death in 1883, in Britain. His book *Capital,* the intellectual basis of modern Communism, is in the main a theoretical analysis of the nature of capitalism. But his evidence was drawn largely from Britain, then the most advanced industrial nation, and his material was largely those Parliamentary Papers criticized, in another of our excerpts, by Professor Ashton. In a few chapters he dealt with the history of capitalism. The bias is obvious. But his view is interesting because its emphasis is upon continuity of economic development: Marx sees the origins of capitalist development in the later Middle Ages. The best book on Marx is the shortest: Isaiah Berlin's *Karl Marx* (1939).

THE ORIGIN of the industrial capitalist was a less gradual affair than that of the farmer. Doubtless many small guild masters, and yet more independent petty artisans or even wage workers, developed into small capitalists; and later (extending by degrees the scale of the exploitation of wage labour, and thus extending accumulation), some of them developed into full-blown capitalists. In the infancy of capitalist production, matters often took much the same course as during the early growth of the medieval town system, when the question which of the runaway serfs should become masters and which should become servants was to a great extent decided by the earlier or later date of their flight. The snail's pace of this method was by no means accordant with the commercial requirements of the new world market created by the great geographical discoveries at the end of the fifteenth century. But the Middle Ages had handed down two distinct forms of capital, ripening under extremely different socio-economic auspices; and both of these, prior to the era when the capitalist method of production became established, ranked as "capital" without qualification. I refer to usurers' capital and merchants' capital.

"At present, all the wealth of society goes first into the possession of the capitalist . . . . He pays the landowner his rent, the labourer his wages, the tax and the tithe gatherer their claims, and keeps a large, indeed the largest, and a continually augmenting share of the annual produce of labour for himself. The capitalist may now be said to be the first owner of all the wealth of the community, though no law has conferred on him the right to this property . . . . This change has been effected by the taking of interest on capital, . . . and it is not a little curious that all the lawgivers of Europe endeavour to prevent this by statutes, viz. statutes against usury . . . . The power of the capitalist over all the wealth

From Karl Marx, *Capital,* Chapter 24, section 6, pp. 831–43, (London, 1930). Translated by Eden and Cedar Paul. Reprinted by permission of George Allen & Unwin Ltd.

of the country is a complete change in the right of property, and by what law, or series of laws, was it effected?" The author would have done well to remember that revolutions are not made by laws.

In the country districts, the feudal structure of society, and in the towns, the guild organization, hindered the transformation of money capital into industrial capital — the transformation of the money capital that had been formed by means of usury and commerce. These hindrances vanished when feudal society was dissolved, when the bands of retainers were broken up, when the countryfolk were expropriated and in part driven off the land. The new manufactures were inaugurated in seaports, or else in parts of the countryside where the old urban system did not run, and where the guilds which were a part of that system had no say. In England, therefore, there was a fierce struggle between the corporate towns and these new industrial nurseries.

The discoveries of gold and silver in America; the extirpation of the indigens in some instances, their enslavement or their entombment in the mines in others; the beginnings of the conquest and looting of the East Indies; the transformation of Africa into a precinct for the supply of the negroes who were the raw material of the slave trade — these were the incidents that characterized the rosy dawn of the era of capitalist production. These were the idyllic processes that formed the chief factors of primary accumulation. Hard upon their heels came the commercial war between the European nations, fought over the whole surface of the globe. It was opened when the Netherlands broke away from Spain; it assumed gigantic proportions in England's anti-Jacobin war; and it found a recent sequel in the opium wars against China.

The various factors of primary accumulation may be classed more or less chronologically, and with special reference to certain countries, such as Spain, Portugal, Holland, France, and England. In the last

named, at the end of the seventeenth century, they were systematically assembled in the colonial system, the national debt system, the modern system of taxation, and the modern system of production. To some extent they rested upon brute force, as, for instance, in the colonial system. One and all, they relied upon the power of the State, upon the concentrated and organized force of society, in order to stimulate the transformation of feudal production into capitalist production, and in order to shorten the period of transition. Force is the midwife of every old society pregnant with a new one. It is itself an economic power.

Writing of the Christian colonial system, W. Howitt, who makes a specialty of Christianity, says: "The barbarities and desperate outrages of the so-called Christian race, throughout every region of the world, and upon every people they have been able to subdue, are not to be paralleled by those of any other race, however fierce, however untaught, and however reckless of mercy and of shame, in any age of the earth." The history of the colonial administration of Holland, the model capitalist nation during the seventeenth century, "is one of the most extraordinary relations of treachery, bribery, massacre, and meanness." Especially characteristic was the system of kidnapping practised at Celebes in order to secure slaves for use in Java. The kidnappers were carefully trained for the purpose. The chief agents in this nefarious trade were the actual thief, the interpreter, and the seller; the main purchasers were the native princes. The young people who were kidnapped were kept in the dungeons of Celebes until they were ready for sending to the slave ships. According to an official report: "This one town of Macassar, e.g., is full of secret prisons, one more horrible than the other, crammed with unfortunates, victims of greed and tyranny, fettered in chains, forcibly torn from their families." Wishing to get possession of Malacca, the Dutch bribed the Portuguese governor of the town, promising to pay him the sum of £21,875 as the price of his treason. When he admitted them within the walls, in the year 1641, as per bargain, they hastened to his house and assassinated him, wishing to "abstain" from payment. Wherever they set foot, devastation and depopulation followed. In 1750, the population of Banjuwangi, a province in Java, was 80,000; by 1811, it had been reduced to 8000. Such are the sweets of commerce!

The English East India Company, as is well known, was not only politically supreme in India, but had an exclusive monopoly of the tea trade, as of the China trade generally, and of the transport of goods to and from Europe. But the coasting trade of India and among the islands, and also the internal trade of India, were a monopoly of the higher officials of the company. The monopolies of salt, opium, betel, and other wares, were inexhaustible mines of wealth. The officials fixed the prices at their own sweet will, and fleeced the unhappy Hindus unmercifully. The governor-general took part in this private traffic. His favourites received contracts under conditions which enabled them, since they were cleverer than the alchemists, to make gold out of nothing. Great fortunes sprang up like mushrooms, primary accumulation going ahead without the original output of so much as a shilling. The report of the impeachment of Warren Hastings is peppered with instances. Here is one. A contract for opium was given to a certain Sullivan when he was just setting out on an official mission to a part of India remote from the districts where opium was grown. He therefore sold his contract to a man named Binn for £40,000. The same day, Binn resold the contract for £60,000. The second buyer, who actually carried out the contract, deposed that he had made vast profits. According to a list laid before parliament, the company and its employees received £6,000,000 from the natives of India as gifts between 1757 and 1766. In the years 1769 and 1770, the English brought about a famine by buying up all the rice and by refusing to sell it again except at fabulous prices.

The treatment of the aborigines was, naturally, worst of all in the plantations which were intended to serve only for export trade, such as the West Indies; and in rich and well populated countries, such as Mexico and India, which were delivered over to plunder. But even in the colonies properly so-called, primary accumulation was true to its Christian character. In 1703, the Puritans of New England, sober virtuosi of Protestantism, by a decree of their assembly, set a premium of £40 upon every Indian scalp and every captured redskin. In 1720, £100 was offered for every scalp. In 1744, when Massachusetts Bay denounced a particular tribe as rebels, the following prices were offered. "For a scalp taken from a male of twelve years and upwards, £100 new currency; for a male prisoner, £105; for females and children taken prisoner, £50; for the scalps of squaws and children, £50." A few decades later, the colonial system took vengeance on the offspring of the pious Pilgrim Fathers, who had revolted against the land of their origin. At English instigation, they were tomahawked by mercenaries in English pay. The British parliament declared bloodhounds and scalping to be "means that God and nature has given into our hand."

Under the influence of the colonial system, commerce and navigation ripened like hothouse fruit. Chartered companies were powerful instruments in promoting the concentration of capital. The colonies provided a market for the rising manufactures, and the monopoly of this market intensified accumulation. The treasures obtained outside Europe by direct looting, enslavement, and murder, flowed to the motherland in streams, and were there turned into capital. Holland, the first country to develop the colonial system to the full, had attained the climax of its commercial greatness as early as the year 1648. It was "in almost exclusive possession of the East India trade and the commerce between the south-east and the north-west of Europe. Its fisheries, its mercantile marine, and its manufactures, surpassed those of any other country. The total capital of the republic probably exceeded that of all the rest of Europe put together." Gülich forgets to add that by 1648 the common folk of Holland were more overworked, more impoverished, and more brutally oppressed than those of all the rest of Europe put together.

To-day, industrial supremacy implies commercial supremacy. In the period of manufacture properly so-called, on the other hand, it was commercial supremacy which implied industrial supremacy. Hence the preponderant role of the colonial system in those days. That system was a "strange god" who had mounted the altar cheek by jowl with the old gods of Europe, and who, one fine day, with a shove and a kick, swept them all into the dustbin. The new god proclaimed the making of surplus value to be the sole end and aim of mankind.

The system of public credit (this meaning the system of national debts), whose early beginnings can be traced in Genoa and Venice before the close of the Middle Ages, spread all over Europe during the manufacturing period. The colonial system, with its seaborne commerce and its trading wars, served as a forcing house. That was why the credit system first struck firm roots in Holland. National debt (i.e. the sale of the State, whether despotic, constitutional, or republican) gives the capitalist era its characteristic stamp. The only part of the so-called national wealth that actually enters into the collective possession of modern peoples is — their national debt. Hence, logically enough, the modern doctrine that a nation grows richer the more deeply it is in debt. Public credit becomes the credo of capital. With the rise of the system of national debt, want of faith in this institution comes to be regarded as the unpardonable sin, the sin against the Holy Ghost.

The public debt becomes one of the most powerful stimuli of primary accumulation. With the wave of an enchanter's wand, "the funds" endow barren money with the power of reproduction, thus transforming it into capital, and this without the risk and the trouble inseparable from its investment in industrial undertakings, and even from putting it out upon usury. The creditors of the State, in actual fact, surrender nothing, for the money that they lend is transformed into public bonds, easily negotiable, bonds which for practical purposes can serve as so much hard cash. Furthermore, the system of national debt has not merely produced, by these means, a class of idle bondholders; has not merely brought into being the improvised wealth of financiers who play the part of middlemen between the government and the nation; has not merely originated the tax farmers, the merchants, and the private manufacturers, to whom a goodly share of every national loan accrues as capital fallen from heaven. In addition, it has given rise to joint-stock companies, to dealings in negotiable securities of all kinds, to stock-jobbing — in a word, to gambling on the stock exchange and to the modern bankocracy.

From the first, the great banks decorated with national titles were merely associations of private speculators, who took up their stand by the side of governments, and, thanks to the privileges they received, were in a position to advance money to the State. Hence the accumulation of the national debt has no more infallible index than the successive increases in the share capital of these banks, whose full development dates from the foundation of the Bank of England in 1694. The Bank of England began by lending its money to the government at 8%. At the same time, it was empowered by parliament to coin money out of this identical capital, by lending it again to the public in the form of banknotes. It was allowed to use these notes for discounting bills, making advances on commodities, and buying the precious metals. Ere long, this credit money of its own manufacture became the medium in which the Bank of England made loans to the State, and paid, on behalf of the State, the interest on the national debt. Nor was it enough that it should thus give with one hand in order to take back with the other, and more than it had given. In addition, while thus receiving, it remained the everlasting creditor of the nation, down to the uttermost farthing. By degrees it inevitably became the keeper of all the gold and silver of the country, and the centre of gravity of all the commercial credit. At about the date when, in England, people gave up the practice of burning witches, they began to hang the forgers of banknotes. The writings of the day, those of Bolingbroke, for instance, show what contemporaries thought of the sudden appearance of this brood of bankocrats, financiers, bondholders, brokers, stock-jobbers, and speculators.

Concurrently with the appearance of the various national debts, there arose an international credit system which often served to hide one of the sources of primary accumulation in this nation or in that. Thus the villainies of the Venetian system of spoliation were a hidden source of the capital wealth of Holland, inasmuch as decaying Venice lent large sums of money to the Dutch. There were similar relations between Holland and England. As early as the beginning of the eighteenth century, the manufactures of Holland had been greatly outstripped by her chief competitor, and she had ceased to be a leading commercial and industrial nation. From 1701 to 1776, therefore, one of the main lines of Dutch business was the lending out of enormous amounts of capital, especially to England, the great rival. The same thing is going on to-day in the relations between England and the United States. A great deal of capital which makes its appearance in the United States without any birth certificate, was yesterday in England the capitalized blood of children.

Since the national debt is buttressed by the public revenue, which must provide whatever sums are needed for the annual payment of interest, etc., the modern system of taxation is a necessary supplement to the system of national loans. The loans enable the government to defray extraordinary expenditure without, for the moment, imposing fresh burdens on the taxpayers; but in the end, higher taxes have to be paid in return for this advantage. On the other hand, the increase in taxation due to the accumulation of the debts that are contracted one after another, makes it necessary for the government to have recourse again and again to fresh loans in order to defray new extraordinary expenses. The modern fiscal system, whose pivot is formed by taxes on the necessaries of life (of course making these dearer), therefore bears within itself the germs of an automatic progression. Excessive taxation is now not so much an incident as a principle. In Holland, where this system was first inaugurated, the noted patriot De Witt extolled it in his *Maxims* as the best system for making the wage earner, submissive, frugal, diligent, and — overburdened with labour. Here, however, we are not so much concerned with the disastrous influence which excessive taxation has upon the position of the wage earner, as upon the way in which it leads to the forcible expropriation of peasants, handicraftsmen, in a word, all the members of the lower middle class. About that there are no two opinions, even among bourgeois economists. The expropriative efficacy of excessive taxation is intensified by the protective system, an integral part thereof.

The undoubted fact that the national debt and the fiscal system which is its handmaid have had a considerable share in bringing about the capitalization of wealth and the expropriation of the masses, has led many writers, such as Cobbett, Doubleday and others, to believe, though wrongly, that this is the chief cause of the poverty of the common people in modern times.

The protective system was an artifice for the making of factory owners, for the expropriation of independent workers, for the capitalization of the national means of production and the national means of subsistence, for forcibly shortening the transition from the medieval to the modern system of production. The various States of Europe scrambled for the patent of this discovery. As soon as they had entered the service of the makers of surplus value, they were not content to fleece their own people, indirectly by protective tariffs, directly by premiums upon export, and the like. In dependent neighbouring countries, industry was forcibly uprooted, as, for example, happened to the woollen manufacture of Ireland under English rule. On the continent of Europe, in accordance with Colbert's prescription, the method was greatly simplified. Here the primary capital of the industrialists was, to a great extent, directly obtained from the State treasury. "Why," asks Mirabeau, "should people go far afield in search of the cause of Saxony's brilliant successes in manufacture before the Seven Years War? National debt, to the tune of a hundred and eighty millions!"

The colonial system, national debt, the heavy burden of taxation, protection, commercial wars, and so on — these offspring of the manufacturing period properly so-called — grew luxuriantly during the childhood of large-scale industry. The birth of the latter was celebrated by a massacre of the innocents; or by its counterpart, a systematic kidnapping of children. Like the royal navy, the factories secured their recruits by means of the press-gang. Inured as Sir F. M. Eden is to the horrors of the expropriation of the countryfolk from the close of the fifteenth century down to his own day (the end of the eighteenth century), prepared though he is complacently to rejoice in this process as "essential" for establishing capitalist agriculture and "the due proportion between arable and pasture land" — he does not show the same amount of economic insight as regards the necessity for the kidnapping of children and their enslavement in order to transform manufacture into machinofacture and to establish the due proportion between capital and labour power. He writes: "It may, perhaps, be worthy the attention of the public to consider, whether in manufacture, which, in order to be carried on successfully, requires that cottages and workhouses should be ransacked for poor children; that they should be employed by turns during the greater part of the night and robbed of that rest which,

though indispensable to all, is most required by the young; and that numbers of both sexes, of different ages and dispositions, should be collected together in such a manner that the contagion of example cannot but lead to profligacy and debauchery; will add to the sum of individual or national felicity."

Now hear Fielden: "In the counties of Derbyshire, Nottinghamshire, and more particularly in Lancashire, the newly invented machinery was used in large factories built on the side of streams capable of turning the water-wheel. Thousands of hands were suddenly required in these places, remote from towns; and Lancashire, in particular, being, till then, comparatively thinly populated and barren, a population was all that she now wanted. The small and nimble fingers of little children being by very far the most in request, the custom instantly sprang up of procuring apprentices from the different parish workhouses of London, Birmingham, and elsewhere. Many, many thousands of these little, hapless creatures were sent down into the north, being from the age of seven to the age of thirteen or fourteen years old. The custom was for the master to clothe his apprentices and to feed and lodge them in an 'apprentice house' near the factory; overseers were appointed to see to the works, whose interest it was to work the children to the utmost, because their pay was in proportion to the quantity of work that they could exact. Cruelty was, of course, the consequence. . . . In many of the manufacturing districts, but particularly, I am afraid, in the guilty county to which I belong (Lancashire), cruelties the most heartrending were practised upon the unoffending and friendless creatures who were thus consigned to the charge of master manufacturers; they were harassed to the brink of death by excess of labour, . . . were flogged, fettered, and tortured in the most exquisite refinement of cruelty; . . . they were in many cases starved to the bone while flogged to their work and . . . even in some instances . . . were driven to commit suicide . . . . The beautiful and romantic valleys of Derbyshire, Nottinghamshire, and Lancashire, secluded from the public eye, became the dismal solitudes of torture, and of many a murder. The profits of manufacturers were enormous; but this only whetted the appetite that it should have satisfied, and therefore the manufacturers had recourse to an expedient that seemed to secure to them those profits without any possibility of limit; they began the practice of what is termed 'night-working,' that is, having tired one set of hands, by working them throughout the day, they had another set ready to go on working throughout the night; the day-set getting into the beds that the night-set had just quitted, and in their turn again, the night-set getting into the beds that the day-set quitted in the morning. It is a common tradition in Lancashire, that the beds never get cold."

With the development of capitalist production in the manufacturing period, the public opinion of Europe had lost the last vestiges of shame and conscience. The nations bragged cynically of every infamy which could serve as a means for the accumulation of capital. Read, for instance, the naive commercial annals of the worthy A. Anderson. Here we find trumpeted forth as a triumph of English statecraft that, when the peace of Utrecht was signed, England, by the Asiento treaty, extorted from the Spaniards the privilege of carrying on the slave trade, hitherto confined as far as the English were concerned to a traffic between the African coast and the English West Indies, between Africa and Spanish America as well. England acquired the monopoly right of supplying Spanish America with 4800 negroes every year until 1743. Simultaneously, this served as an official cover for British smuggling. It was upon the foundation of the slave trade that Liverpool became a great city, for there the slave trade was the method of primary accumulation. Almost down to our own day, there have been "respectable" citizens of Liverpool ready to write enthusiastically about the slave trade. See, for instance, Dr. Aikin's already quoted work, written in 1795, where he speaks of "that spirit of bold adventure which has characterized the trade of Liverpool, and rapidly carried it to its present state of prosperity; has occasioned vast employment for shipping and sailors, and greatly augmented the demand for the manufactures of the country." In the year 1730, Liverpool had 15 bottoms employed in the slave trade; in 1751, there were 53; in 1760, there were 74; in 1770, there were 96; and in 1792, there were 132.

The cotton industry, while introducing child slavery into England, gave at the same time an impetus towards the transformation of the slave system of the United States, which had hitherto been a more or less patriarchal one, into a commercial system of exploitation. Speaking generally, the veiled slavery of the European wage earners became the pedestal of unqualified slavery in the New World.

So much pains did it cost to establish the "eternal natural laws" of the capitalist method of production, to complete the divorce of the workers from the means of labour, to transform at one pole the social means of production and the social means of subsistence into capital, while transforming at the other pole the masses of the population into wage workers, into free "labouring poor," that artificial product of modern history. As Augier said, money "comes into the world with a birthmark on the cheek"; it is no less true that capital comes into the world soiled with mire from top to toe, and oozing blood from every pore.

THE INDUSTRIAL REVOLUTION:
The Rulers and the Masses

JOHN L. AND BARBARA HAMMOND

Both Oxford-educated, the Hammonds did most of their work together, and they are famous for the series of books on the Industrial Revolution and its social effects. Over the general reader in England, the sway of their interpretation is still undisputed. Among scholars, they are heavily attacked, not for factual inaccuracy but for the lack of balance inherent in their emphasis on cultural and moral questions, and in their intense sympathy for victims of hardship or oppression. J. L. Hammond died in 1949.

ROME imported slaves to work in Italy: Englishmen counted it one of the advantages of the slave trade that it discouraged the competition of British colonists with British manufacturers. For the slaves were chiefly needed for industries like sugar planting, in which Englishmen at home were not engaged. Thus it might be argued that England had escaped the fate of Rome and that she so used the slave trade as to make it a stimulus rather than a discouragement to native energy and skill.

Yet England did not escape the penalty. For it was under this shadow that the new industrial system took form and grew, and the immense power with which invention had armed mankind was exercised at first under conditions that reproduced the degradation of the slave trade. The factory system was not like war or revolution a deliberate attack on society: it was the effort of men to use will, energy, organization and intelligence for the service of man's needs. But in adapting this new power to the satisfaction of its wants England could not escape from the moral atmosphere of the slave trade: the atmosphere in which it was the fashion to think of men as things.

In the days of the guilds the workman was regarded as a person with some kind of property or status; the stages by which this character is restricted to a smaller and smaller part of the working classes, and more and more of the journeymen and apprentices fall into a permanently inferior class have been described by historians. In the early nineteenth century the workers, as a class, were looked upon as so much labour power to be used at the discretion of, and under conditions imposed by, their masters; not as men and women who are entitled to some voice in the arrangements of their life and work. The use of child labour on a vast scale had an important bearing on the growth of this temper.

The children of the poor were regarded as workers long before the Industrial Revolution. Locke suggested that they should begin work at three; Defoe rejoiced to see that in the busy homes of the Yorkshire clothiers "scarce anything above four years old, but its hands were sufficient for its own

From John L. and Barbara Hammond, *The Rise of Modern Industry*, (London, 1925). Chapters 12 and 13, pp. 194–5, 196–9, 200–201, 203–8, 210, 211–3, 217, 218, 219–20, 222–4, 226–32. By permission of Mrs. Barbara Hammond and Methuen & Co. Ltd.

support." The new industrial system provided a great field for the employment of children, and Pitt himself, speaking in 1796, dwelt on this prospect with a satisfaction strange to modern minds, and disturbing even to some who heard him. One of the most elaborate of all Bentham's fantasies was his scheme for a great series of Industry Houses, 250 in number, each to hold 2,000 persons, for whose work, recreation, education, and marriage most minute regulations were laid down. An advantage he claimed for his system was that it would enable the apprentices to marry at "the earliest period compatible with health," and this was made possible by the employment of children. "And to what would they be indebted for this gentlest of all revolutions? To what, but to economy? Which dreads no longer the multiplication of man, now that she has shown by what secure and unperishable means infant man, a drug at present so much worse than worthless, may be endowed with an indubitable and universal value." Infant man soon became in the new industrial system what he never was in the old, the basis of a complicated economy.

Most children under the old domestic system worked at home under their parents' eyes, but in addition to such children there were workhouse children, who were hired out by overseers to every kind of master or mistress. Little care was taken to see that they were taught a trade or treated with humanity by their employers, and though London magistrates like Fielding did what they could to protect this unhappy class, their state was often a kind of slavery. The number of children on the hands of the London parishes was largely increased in the latter part of the eighteenth century, because an Act of Parliament, passed in 1767 in consequence of the exertions of Jonas Hanway, compelled the London parishes to board out their young children, and to give a bonus to every nurse whose charge survived. Until this time very few parish pauper children grew up to trouble their betters.

The needs of the London workhouses on the one hand, and those of the factory on the other, created a situation painfully like the situation in the West Indies. The Spanish employers in America wanted outside labour, because the supply of native labour was deficient in quantity and quality. The new cotton mills placed on streams in solitary districts were in the same case. The inventions had found immense scope for child labour, and in these districts there were only scattered populations. In the workhouses of large towns there was a quantity of child labour available for employment, that was even more powerless and passive in the hands of a master than the stolen negro, brought from his burning home to the hold of a British slave ship. Of these children it could be said, as it was said of the negroes, that their life at best was a hard one, and that their choice was often the choice between one kind of slavery and another. So the new industry which was to give the English people such immense power in the world borrowed at its origin from the methods of the American settlements.

How closely the apologies for this child serf system followed the apologies for the slave trade can be seen from Romilly's description of a speech made in the House of Commons in 1811. "Mr. Wortley, who spoke on the same side, insisted that, although in the higher ranks of society it was true that to cultivate the affections of children for their family was the source of every virtue, yet that it was not so among the lower orders, and that it was a benefit to take them away from their miserable and depraved parents. He said too that it would be highly injurious to the public to put a stop to the binding of so many apprentices to the cotton manufacturers, as it must necessarily raise the price of labour and enhance the price of cotton manufactured goods."

It was not until 1816 that Parliament would consent to reform this system of transportation. In that year a Bill that had been repeatedly introduced by Mr. Wilbraham Bootle passed both Houses, and it was made illegal for London children to be apprenticed more than forty miles away from their parish. But by this time the problem had changed, for steam-power had superseded water-power and mills could be built in towns; in these towns there were parents who were driven by poverty to send their children to the mills. In the early days of the factory system there had been a prejudice against sending children to the mill, but the hand-loom weaver had been sinking steadily from the beginning of the century into deeper and deeper poverty, and he was no longer able to maintain himself and his family. Sometimes too an adult worker was only given work on condition that he send his child to the mill. Thus the apprentice system was no longer needed. It had carried the factories over the first stage and at the second they could draw on the population of the neighbourhood.

These children, who were commonly called "free-labour children," were employed from a very early age. Most of them were piecers: that is they had to join together or piece the threads broken in the several roving or spinning machines. But there were tasks less skilled than these, and Robert Owen said that many children who were four or five years old were set to pick up waste cotton on the floor. Their hours were those of the apprentice children. They entered the mill gates at five or six in the morning and left them again at seven or eight at night. They had half an hour for breakfast and an hour for dinner, but even during meal hours they were often at work cleaning a standing machine; Fielden calculated that a child following the spinning machine could walk twenty miles in the twelve hours. Oastler was once in the company of a West Indian slave-master and three Bradford spinners. When the slave-master heard what were the children's hours he declared: "I have always thought myself disgraced by being the owner of slaves, but we never in the West Indies thought it possible for any human being to be so cruel as to require a child of nine

years old to work twelve and a half hours a day."

This terrible evil fastened itself on English life as the other fastened itself on the life of the Colonies. Reformers had an uphill struggle to get rid of its worst abuses. Throughout this long struggle the apologies for child labour were precisely the same as the apologies for the slave trade. Cobbett put it in 1833 that the opponents of the Ten Hours Bill had discovered that England's manufacturing supremacy depended on 30,000 little girls. This was no travesty of their argument. The champions of the slave trade pointed to the £70,000,000 invested in the sugar plantations, to the dependence of our navy on our commerce, and to the dependence of our commerce on the slave trade. This was the argument of Chatham in one generation and Rodney in another. When Fox destroyed the trade in 1806 even Sir Robert Peel complained that we were philosophizing when our looms were idle, and George Rose, that the Americans would take up the trade, and that Manchester, Stockport and Paisley would starve. They could point to Liverpool, which had been turned from a small hamlet into a flourishing port by the trade. For Liverpool was the centre of the commerce that throve on this trade. She shipped Manchester goods to Africa, took thence slave cargoes to the West Indies and brought back sugar and raw cotton. In the eleven years from 1783 to 1793 Liverpool slaving ships carried over 300,000 slaves from Africa to the West Indies and sold them for over £15,000,000. In 1793 this single port had secured three-sevenths of the slave trade of Europe. A Liverpool Member said that nobody would introduce the slave trade, but that so large a body of interests and property now depended on it that no equitable person would abolish it.

The argument for child labour followed the same line. In the one case the interests of Liverpool, in the other those of Lancashire, demanded of the nation that it should accept one evil in order to escape from another. Cardwell, afterwards the famous army reformer, talked of the great capital sunk in the cotton industry and the danger of the blind impulse of humanity. Sir James Graham thought that the Ten Hours Bill would ruin the cotton industry and with it the trade of the country. The cotton industry had taken the place in this argument that had been held by the navy in the earlier controversy. Our population, which had grown so rapidly in the Industrial Revolution, was no longer able to feed itself: the food it bought was paid for by its manufactures: those manufactures depended on capital: capital depended on profits: profits depended on the labour of the boys and girls who enabled the manufacturer to work his mills long enough at a time to repay the cost of the plant and to compete with his foreign rivals. This was the circle in which the nation found its conscience entangled.

The life of man had been regulated before by the needs of a particular order or the pattern of a particular society: the government of king or church or lord had defined narrow limits within which a man was to run his course. The new master was a world force, for this economy could make its profits, so it was believed, where it chose, and when Englishmen rebelled against its rule it would seek its gains and bestow its blessings elsewhere. This way of looking at the new industrial system put man at the mercy of his machines, for if the new power was not made man's servant, it was bound to become his master. If at every point the governing claim was not man's good but the needs of the machine, it was inevitable that man's life and the quality of his civilization should be subordinated to this great system of production.

Nobody could argue that the ordinary worker before the Industrial Revolution was a free man, whether he was a peasant in the country or a journeyman in the town, but the age which watched the change from domestic to factory industry in Lancashire and Yorkshire could see that a great many men and women lost what they had possessed of initiative and choice.

For the Industrial Revolution gave a look of catastrophe to the final stages of a process that had been in train for centuries. Before this time there had been fierce quarrels between master and journeyman. Professor Unwin describes a scene at Chester in 1358 when the master weavers, shearmen and challoners and walkers attacked their journeymen with iron-pointed poles during the Corpus Christi procession. It is true, as he says, that from the middle of the fourteenth century there was to be found in every industrial centre of Western Europe a body of workmen in every craft who had no prospect before them but that of remaining journeymen all their lives, that there was constant friction between this class and the masters, and perpetual disputes over hours, wages and other conditions. The Industrial Revolution did not create the quarrels of class, nor did it create the wrongs and discontents that are inevitable in any relationship, where interests are sharply opposed and power is mismatched. But it made the disproportion of power much greater, and the immense extension of industrial life which followed came at a time when there was a general disposition to regard the working-class world as idle and profligate, and to regard industry as a system that served men by ruling them. Consequently the Industrial Revolution, if it did not introduce all the evils that were so acute in the new factories, gave them a far greater range and importance.

What happened at the Industrial Revolution was that all the restraints that the law imposed on workmen in particular industries, were standardized into a general law for the whole of the expanding world of industry, and all the regulations and laws that recognized him as a person with rights were withdrawn or became inoperative. The workman, as we have seen, lost one by one the several Acts of Parliament that gave him protection from his master in this or that industry. His personal liberty was circumscribed by a series of Acts, beginning with the Act of 1719, which made it a crime for him to take his wits and his skills into another country: a law that applied to the artisan but not to the inventor. At the end of the century the masters were given complete control of their workmen, by a Combination Act which went far beyond the Acts against combinations already on the Statute book. By the Combination Act of 1799 any workman who combined with any other workman to seek an improvement in his working conditions was liable to be brought before a single magistrate — it might be his own employer — and sent to prison for three months. This Act, the chief authors of which were Pitt and Wilberforce, was modified next year, when Parliament decided that two magistrates were necessary to form a court, and that a magistrate who was a master in the trade affected should not try offences, but these modifications did not affect in practice the power that the law gave to employers. Under cover of this Act it often happened that a master would threaten his workman with imprisonment or service in the fleet in order to compel him to accept the wages he chose to offer. In 1824 Place and Hume, taking advantage of the reaction from the worst of the panics produced by the French Revolution, managed to carry the repeal of the Combination Laws. Next year, after their repeal had been celebrated by an outburst of strikes, a less stringent law was put in their place. But the view of the new system as a beneficent mechanism which the mass of men must serve with a blind and unquestioning obedience was firmly rooted in the temper of the time, and thus anyone who tried to think of Englishmen in the spirit of Burke's description of a man, found himself strangely out of tune in a world where the workman was refused education, political rights and any voice in the conditions of his employment.

"At Tyldesley," it was said in a pamphlet published during a strike, "they work fourteen hours per day, including the nominal hour for dinner; the door is locked in working hours, except half an hour at tea time; the workpeople are not allowed to send for water to drink, in the hot factory: and even the rain water is locked up, by the master's order, otherwise they would be happy to drink even that." In this mill a shilling fine was inflicted on a spinner found dirty, or found washing, heard whistling or found with his window open in a temperature of 84 degrees. The men who were thrust into this discipline, however hard and bare their lives, had been accustomed to work in their own homes at their own time. The sense of servitude that was impressed on the age by this discipline, by the methods of government, the look of the towns and the absence of choice or initiative in the lives of the mass of the workpeople, was strengthened by the spectacle of the new power. "While the engine runs," wrote an observer, "the people must work — men, women and children yoked together with iron and steam. The animal machine — breakable in the best case, subject to a thousand sources of suffering — is chained fast to the iron machine which knows no suffering and no weariness."

"Two centuries ago not one person in a thousand wore stockings; one century ago not one person in five hundred wore them; now not one person in a thousand is without them." This sentence from *The Results of Machinery* (1831), one of the publications of the Society for the Diffusion of Useful Knowledge, illustrates a feature of the Industrial Revolution that made a profound impression on the imagination of the time. When capital was applied to production on a large scale, it gained its profits by producing in bulk; producing, that is, for mass consumption. Energy and brains were now devoted to satisfying, not the luxurious taste of the classes that were served by the commerce of medieval Europe, but the needs of the poor consumer.

It was natural for the age that witnessed the first triumphs of the new system to worship production for profit. This great addition to the wealth of the world seemed to follow automatically when men were left to acquire at their pleasure. Swift success is a dazzling spectacle, and the new industrial system provided a new miracle every day. A visitor to a mill in Bolton or Preston watching the inventions of Crompton, Hargreaves, Arkwright and Watt, stood before a power that was conquering the world as no Caesar or Napoleon had ever conquered it. To the generation that saw on the one hand the small farmer carrying the wool he had woven on his hand-loom at home to Leeds or Halifax on the back of his horse, and on the other the great mills at Blackburn or Rochdale sending out thousands of bales of cotton to be transported by rail and ship to the other ends of the earth, it looked as if progress that had dawdled through so many centuries was, now that man had learnt its simple secret, to follow a rapid and unbroken course; as if the society that surrendered itself to the control of private profit released a force that would regenerate the world. Any people into whose hands this power had fallen would probably have been plunged into the state described by Boulton as "steam-mill mad," just as any people that had first grasped the new wealth of America in the fifteenth century would have been as frantic as the Spaniards for gold and silver.

The English people, from the whole tone and cast of its thought and politics, was specially liable to be swept off its balance by this revolution. The positive enthusiasms of the time were for science and progress: for material development and individual liberty. The restraints of custom, tradition and religion had never been so frail over the classes that held power. In the Middle Ages the Church had laid a controlling or checking hand on manners: the Guilds had hampered individual enterprise by a corporate discipline. But the Church of the eighteenth century was merely part of the civil order, without standards, authority or conscience of its own; the Guilds were dead, and their successors stood not for corporate spirit, but for property and nothing else. Thus neither Church nor Guild survived to offer any obstacle to the view that headlong wealth was the sovereign

good for society and for the individual, for cities and for men.

This view was powerfully encouraged by the philosophy of confidence which the eighteenth century had substituted for a religion of awe. Medieval religion had watched man's instincts with anxious eyes, as instincts needing to be disciplined, coerced, held fast by Pope and priest; the Puritans, though they gave him different masters, were not less suspicious of the natural man. The new philosophy, on the other hand, regarded man's instincts as the best guide to conduct, and taught that left to himself man so acted as to serve rather than injure the society to which he belonged. Capital was a magical power; man was a benevolent creature. Thus so far as an age lives by a system of belief, this age drew its wisdom from a philosophy that found nothing but good in the new force to which it had submitted.

The state of politics was also congenial to this impulse. Neither Conservative nor Radical offered any distracting or competing motive, for while they disagreed about political and administrative reform, they did not disagree about the advantages of a system under which acquisition and profit-making were unimpeded. If it was the manufacturers who promoted the new system in industry, the landowners were equally active in promoting it on their estates. The most important force in making the English an industrial people was the destruction of the village. Nations that kept the peasant could never be completely absorbed in the new industrial system, and it was the landowner, often of course the new landowner, who had come from the world of finance and industry, who pushed the English peasant out.

England was on the eve of a great expansion of resources, numbers, wealth and power. What were the new towns to be like? What their schools, their pleasures, their houses, their standards of a good life, their plans for co-operation and fellowship? What the fate of the mass of people who did not feel or force their way through the doors thrown open to enterprise? To all these questions the Industrial Revolution gave the same answer: "Ask Capital." And neither Conservative nor Radical, the man defending or the man attacking bad laws and bad customs, thought that answer wrong. But that answer meant that the age had turned aside from making a society in order to make a system of production.

The effect of this concentration is seen in the towns of the age. They were left, like everything else, to the mercy and direction of the spirit of profit. Mankind did not admire wealth for the first time; but the rich merchant of Bruges, Genoa or Norwich, like the rich Pope or the rich noble of the Middle Ages, or the rich Senator of the Roman Empire, had regarded the beauty and culture of his town as a sign of his own importance and success. Vespasian, frugal as he was, did not hesitate to begin the restoration of the Capitol, though he had inherited a debt of over three hundred million pounds. The private citizen who gave Bordeaux an aqueduct costing £160,000, or the benefactor who spent £80,000 on the walls of Marseilles, the soldier who provided free baths for slave girls at Suessa Senonum, the civic dignitaries who gave temples and theatres, these typical figures of the early Roman Empire would have been astonished to learn that in the districts of South Wales, where men had risen in a few years to such wealth as would have rivalled the wealth of Atticus or Herodes, the poorer classes had to go a mile for water, waiting in a queue a great part of the night; that the chief town of this rich district had neither public lighting nor drainage.

Yet the Industrial Revolution which had given these men their fortunes had made it much easier to supply the needs of the towns that sprang up beside their great establishments. One of the products of that revolution was gas lighting; the Soho Works were lighted with gas in 1802 to celebrate the Peace of Amiens. Great factories at Manchester and Leeds soon followed the example of Boulton and Watt.

Another product was the cheap water-pipe. At the end of the American War English ironmasters were exporting water-pipes to Paris and New York. The Romans had no cheap water-pipes made by the help of mechanical power, but they could supply their towns with clean water, whereas the people of Merthyr Tydfil, their streets echoing by day and night with the clamour of forge and furnace, had to drink whatever the river brought them.

The rage for production had swept England, as the rage for piety had swept the age of the monarchists. And production had taken a form that was intensely isolating; the successful man kept his secrets, tried to find his neighbours' secrets, strove for personal gain, took personal risks, made his way by personal initiative and personal enterprise.

This concentration led to the complete neglect of the most urgent tasks of the age. In the first twenty years of the nineteenth century the population of Manchester increased from 94,000 to 160,000; of Bolton from 29,000 to 50,000; Leeds more than doubled its population between 1801 and 1831; Bradford, which had 23,000 inhabitants in 1831, grew grass in its streets at the end of the eighteenth century. Oldham, which had 38,000 inhabitants in 1821, had three or four hundred in 1760. In the twenty years from 1801 to 1821 the population of Lancashire grew from 672,000 to 1,052,000; in the next twenty years it grew to 1,701,000. The population of Merthyr increased from 7,700 to 35,000 between 1801 and 1841, and that of the two counties of Glamorgan and Monmouth from 126,000 to 305,000. Industry was accumulating dense masses of people into particular districts, where the workman was shut up in melancholy streets, without gardens or orchards. England was passing from a country to a town life, as she passed from a peasant to an industrial civilization. What this meant is clear if we compare the state of the towns as revealed in the health statistics, with that of the country districts. In 1757 Dr. Percival put the death-rate for

Manchester at 1 in 25, for Liverpool at 1 in 27. In Monton, a few miles from Manchester, the ratio was at that time 1 in 68, at Horwich, between Bolton and Chorley, 1 in 66, at Darwen, three miles from Blackburn, 1 in 56. The Industrial Revolution was to spread the conditions of town life over places like Monton, Horwich and Darwen.

The problem of arranging and controlling the expansion of the towns was thus the most urgent of the problems created by the Industrial Revolution. Its importance was illustrated by a picture of some cottages near Preston published by the Health of Towns Commission in 1844. These cottages stood in two rows, separated by little back yards, with an open sewer running the whole length. The picture was given as an example of dangerous and disgusting drainage. But this is not its chief significance. One would suppose that these huddled cottages, without gardens of any kind, were built in a crowded town, where not an inch of space was available for amenities. They were in fact in the open country. Clearly then there was more here than a problem of drainage, for if it was left to private enterprise to develop this district, under the guidance of an uncontrolled sense for profit, these rows would spring up all round, and Preston would have another slum on her hands. This is what happened in the new industrial districts. When the Health of Towns Commission investigated towns like Manchester, they were told that the worst evils were not the evils of the past, for new Manchester was reproducing the slums and alleys of the old, and spreading them, of course, over a far wider surface. Of no other problem was it so true that neglect by one generation tied the hands and the mind of the next.

In 1840 a Committee of the House of Commons recommended a series of reforms of a drastic and far-reaching character, and the Government of the day, represented at the Home Office by Normanby, a minister who was in earnest, introduced Bills to give effect to its proposals. This Committee regretted that there was no general building law in force at the beginning of the century, "the fulfilment of one of the first duties of a humane government," and called for a general building law, a general sewage law, the setting up of a Board of Health in every town, with instructions to look after water supply, burial grounds, open spaces and slums. Cellar dwellings and back-to-back houses were to be forbidden. The importance of preserving amenities, footpaths, and something of the look of the country was impressed on Parliament. The most significant comment of the neglect of these proposals is to be found in the recurring complaint that runs through all the Reports on Health and Housing that were issued in the nineteenth century. Town planning never found its way into an Act of Parliament until the twentieth century, and back-to-back houses (made illegal in 1909) were built in great numbers two generations after Normanby's Bill had proposed to forbid them. The Commission which sat in 1867 found in existence the main evils that were revealed by the Committee of 1840; the Commission of 1884 found in existence the main evils that had been revealed by the Commission of 1867. In many towns the death-rate was higher in 1867 than in 1842, and Cross, speaking as Home Secretary in 1871, could match the terrible revelations by which Chadwick had tried to rouse the indignation and fear of the Parliaments of Melbourne and Peel.

Before each Commission the large towns disclosed the same difficulties. The law did not enable them to control expansion, or to prevent the creation on their circumference of the evils they were trying to suppress at the centre. The Committee of 1840 had pointed out that back-to-back houses were being introduced into towns that had been free from them. Town Clerks told the Commission of 1867 that whole streets were still being built on "a foundation composed of old sweepings, refuse from factories, old buildings and other objectionable matter." Parliament passed Public Health Acts and set up authorities with sharply limited powers, but the fatal blindness to the character of the problem, as a problem in the organization and planning of town life, which marked the early phases of the Industrial Revolution, persisted. England learnt sooner than other countries how to cleanse her towns, but towns still continued to grow at the pleasure of the profit seeker. Each generation looked wistfully back to its predecessor as living in a time when the evil was still manageable, and over the reforms of the century could be inscribed the motto "the Clock that always loses." For the creed of the first age of the Industrial Revolution, that the needs of production must regulate the conditions of life, and that the incidence of profits must decide in what kind of town, in what kind of streets, and in what kind of houses a nation shall find its home, had cast its melancholy fatalism over the mind of the generations that followed. The trouble was not merely that the evil was greater when a town had a quarter of a million of inhabitants instead of a hundred thousand. It was that men still saw with the eyes of their grandfathers, and that they were busy polishing the life of the slum, when a race that was free and vigorous in its mind could have put an end to it. With the consequences and the traditions of this neglect industrial civilization is still fighting an up-hill battle.

The other task that became immensely more important with the Industrial Revolution was the task of education. Adam Smith had pointed out that the division of labour, though good for production, was bad for the mind of the labourer. Men, women and children lost range, diversity and incentive in their work, when that work was simplified to a single process, or a monotonous routine. Life was more versatile and interesting when craftsmanship was combined with agriculture. Under the new system a boy or youth learnt one process and one process only; a great part of his mind was never exercised; many of his faculties remained idle and undeveloped. Moreover, apprenticeship was declining, and thus an important method of education was passing out of fashion.

Nor were these the only reasons why popular education was needed more urgently in this than in previous ages. Men learn from their leisure as well as from their work. Now the common life of the time was singularly wanting in inspiration, comparing in this respect unfavourably with the life of the ancient or that of the medieval world. The Greeks and the Romans put a great deal of beauty into their public buildings; they made provision, in some cases barbarous provision, for public amusement; they did not isolate art and pleasure for the delight of a small class. Life in Manchester or Merthyr was very different. Mr. and Mrs. Webb, who have described the work of the several bodies of Improvement Commissioners at this time, remark that even the most energetic among them made no provision for parks, open spaces, libraries, picture galleries, museums, baths, or any kind of education. The workmen put it that their sports had been converted into crimes, and their holidays into fast days. Rich men in the Roman Empire spent their money on things that were for common enjoyment as rich men in the Middle Ages spent their money on things that were for common salvation. Pliny gave to his native Como, a library, a school endowment, a foundation for the nurture of poor children and a Temple of Ceres with spacious colonnades to shelter the traders who visited the great fair. The wealthy Herodes Atticus, tutor of Marcus Aurelius, gave a theatre to Athens with a roof of cedar to hold 6,000 persons, another theatre to Corinth, and a race-course to Delphi. Such gifts were common in the days of the Antonines. But in the England of the early Industrial Revolution all diversions were regarded as wrong, because it was believed that successful production demanded long hours, a bare life, a mind without temptation to think or to remember, to look before or behind. Some Lancashire magistrates used to refuse on this ground to license public-houses where concerts were held. Long hours did not begin with the Industrial Revolution, but in the Middle Ages the monotony of industrial work was broken for the journeyman by frequent holidays, saints' days and festivals; for medieval Europe, like Rome, gave some place in common life to the satisfaction of the imagination and the senses.

Perhaps nothing served so directly to embitter the relations of class in the Industrial Revolution as this fashionable view, that the less amusement the worker had, the better. The love of amusement has a place of special significance in the English character. If the English workman stints himself for his holiday week at Blackpool, as the Scottish peasant stints himself to send his son into the Ministry, or the Irish or French peasant stints himself to own a little property, it is not merely because he sets his holiday high among the enjoyments of life. The satisfaction of this desire is connected with his self-respect. The football field and the holiday resort represent a world in which the poor man feels himself the equal of the rich: a corner of life in which he has not bargained away any rights or liberties. It might be said of the early Radicals, that they sought to extend to his view of politics, and of the early Socialists, that they sought to extend to his views of property, the spirit that ruled the workman's outlook on his pleasures: that they sought to make him resent in those spheres the inequalities he was so quick to resent, when employer or magistrate tried to keep from him amusements that other classes enjoyed.

The need for popular education became in these circumstances specially urgent. The reading of print is one way of using and exercising the mind, and its value at any moment depends on circumstances. In the days of pageants and spectacles, when story-tellers went from village to village, when pedlars and pilgrims brought tales of adventure or war or the habits of foreign countries, a man might be unable to read

or write, and yet take a share in the culture of the time. Buildings, plays, music, these may be greater influences on the mind than book or pamphlet or newspaper. But the youth of the early nineteenth century who found no scope for initiative or experiment or design in his work, found no stimulus or education for his fancy from the spectacles and amusements provided for his recreation. Science was improving the mechanical contrivances of life, but the arts of life were in decline. To take advantage of these improvements, the power to read and write was essential. In a world depending on newspapers, the man who cannot read lives in the darkest exile; when the factory was taking the place of the craft, the newspaper the place of the pageant, illiteracy was the worst disfranchisement a man could suffer.

Horner, reporting in 1839 that a population of over a hundred thousand persons in a district of Lancashire comprising Oldham and Ashton was without a single public day-school for poor scholars, the Commissioner who said of South Wales in 1842 that not one grown male in fifty could read, both spoke of an age in which the story-teller had left the village, and the apprenticeship system was leaving the town. Adam Smith had argued that as the division of labour deprived the worker of opportunities of training his mind, the State ought to provide opportunities by public education. The ruling class argued, on the contrary, that with the new methods of specialization, industry could not spare a single hour for the needs of the men who served it. In such a system education had no place. The great majority of the ruling class believed, as one of them put it, that the question to ask was not whether education would develop a child's faculties for happiness and citizenship, but whether it "would make him a good servant in agriculture and other laborious employments to which his rank in society had destined him."

Thus England asked for profits and received profits. Everything turned to profit. The towns had their profitable dirt, their profitable smoke, their profitable slums, their profitable disorder, their profitable ignorance, their profitable despair. The curse of Midas was on this society: on its corporate life, on its common mind, on the decisive and impatient step it had taken from the peasant to the industrial age. For the new town was not a home where man could find beauty, happiness, leisure, learning, religion, the influences that civilize outlook and habit, but a bare and desolate place, without colour, air or laughter, where man, woman and child worked, ate and slept. This was to be the lot of the mass of mankind: this the sullen rhythm of their lives. The new factories and the new furnaces were like the Pyramids, telling of man's enslavement, rather than of his power, casting their long shadow over the society that took such pride in them.

WORKERS' LIVING STANDARDS
A Modern Revision

THOMAS S. ASHTON

Professor first at Manchester and then at London University, T. S. Ashton is the foremost living authority on the period which some of us still call The Industrial Revolution. A series of monographs (listed at the end of this book) was supplemented in 1948 by *The Industrial Revolution*, which looks like a tiny textbook but is in fact a brilliant essay, full of original research and challenging views. On the eve of retirement from teaching, Professor Ashton published *Economic History of England, The 18th Century*. The excerpts which follow constitute a plea for considering the Industrial Revolution in economic rather than in moral terms, for understanding the practical difficulties of men meeting new situations with old ideas and institutions, and for re-assessing evidence some of which is by its very nature one-sided.

To occupy a chair of economic history in the University of London means that, instead of being able to give one's vacation to the refreshment of body and spirit or to the pursuit of knowledge, one is forced to spend much of it in reading examination scripts produced not only by one's own students but also by several hundred young men and women in all parts of Britain and, indeed, in the uttermost parts of the earth. This situation is unenviable. But at least it enables one to speak with assurance about the ideas held about the economic past by those who, in a short time, will be holding positions of authority in industry, commerce, journalism, politics, and administration and will therefore be influential in forming what we call "public opinion."

It is a truism that men's political and economic ideas depend as much on the experiences of the preceding generation as on the needs of their own. Asked by Lionel Robbins what they considered to be the outstanding problem of today, the majority of a class of students at the School of Economics answered unhesitatingly, "To maintain full employment." After a decade of full, or overfull, employment in England, the shadow of the 1930's hides from large numbers the real problems of postwar England. There is, however, a deeper shadow that obscures reality and darkens counsels. It is cast by the grievances — real or alleged — of workingmen who lived and died a century ago. According to a large number of the scripts which it has been my lot to read, the course of English history since about the year 1760 to the setting-up of the welfare state in 1945 was marked by little but toil and sweat and oppression. Economic forces, it would appear, are by nature malevolent. Every labour-saving device has led to a decline of skill and to

From Thomas S. Ashton, "The Treatment of Capitalism by Historians," in *Capitalism and the Historians* edited by Friedrich A. Hayek, (Chicago, 1954), pp. 33–43, 50–4, 62–3; and from *The Industrial Revolution*, (London, 1948), pp. 149–61. By permission of The University of Chicago Press, Routledge & Kegan Paul Ltd., and the Oxford University Press.

an increase of unemployment. Is it not well known that, when prices rise, wages lag behind, and the standard of life of the workers falls? But what if prices fall? Is it not equally well known that this must result in a depression of trade and industry, a fall of wages and unemployment, so that, once more, the standard of life of the workers falls?

Modern youth is prone to melancholy; like Rachel, it refuses to be comforted. Yet I think it is something more than adolescent pessimism that is responsible for this climate of opinion. Students attend lectures and read textbooks, and it is a matter of common prudence to pay some heed to what they have heard and read. A good deal — indeed, far too much — of what appears in the scripts is literal reproduction of the spoken or written word. Much the greater part of the responsibility must lie with the professional economic historian.

The student of English economic history is fortunate in having at his disposal the reports of a long series of Royal Commissions and Committees of Inquiry beginning in the eighteenth century but reaching full stream in the 1830's, 1840's, and 1850's. These reports are one of the glories of the Victorian age. They signalized a quickening of social conscience, a sensitiveness to distress, that had not been evident in any other period or in any other country. Scores of massive folios provided statistical and verbal evidence that all was not well with large numbers of the people of England and called the attention of legislators and the reading public to the need for reform. The economic historians of the succeeding generations could do no other than draw on their findings; and scholarship, no less than society, benefited. There was, however, loss as well as gain. A picture of the economic system constructed from Blue Books dealing with social grievances, and not with the normal processes of economic development, was bound to be one-sided. It is such a picture of early Victorian society that has become fixed in the minds of popular writers and is reproduced in my

scripts. A careful reading of the reports would, indeed, lead to the conclusion that much that was wrong was the result of laws, customs, habits, and forms of organization that belonged to earlier periods and were rapidly becoming obsolete. It would have brought home to the mind that it was not among the factory employees but among the domestic workers, whose traditions and methods were those of the eighteenth century, that earnings were at their lowest. It would have provided evidence that it was not in the large establishments making use of steam power but in the garret or cellar workshops that conditions of employment were at their worst. It would have led to the conclusion that it was not in the growing manufacturing towns or the developing coalfields but in remote villages and the countryside that restrictions on personal freedom and the evils of truck were most marked. But few had the patience to go carefully through these massive volumes. It was so much easier to pick out the more sensational evidences of distress and work them into a dramatic story of exploitation. The result has been that a generation that had the enterprise and industry to assemble the facts, the honesty to reveal them, and the energy to set about the task of reform has been held up to obloquy as the author, not of the Blue Books, but of the evils themselves. Conditions in the mills and the factory town were so bad, it seemed, that there must have been deterioration; and, since the supposed deterioration had taken place at a time when machinery had increased, the machines, and those who owned them, must have been responsible.

At the same time the romantic revival in literature led to an idyllic view of the life of the present. The idea that agriculture is the only natural and healthy activity for human beings has persisted, and indeed spread, as more of us have escaped from the curse of Adam — or, as the tedious phrase goes, "become divorced from the soil." A year ago an examinee remarked profoundly that "in earlier centuries agriculture was widespread in England" but added sorrowfully, "Today it is confined to the rural areas." There was a similar idealization of the condition of the domestic worker, who had taken only the first step in the proceedings for divorce. Bear with me while I read some passages with which Engels (who is usually acclaimed a realist) opens his account of *The Condition of the Working Classes in England in 1844*. It is, of course, based on the writings of the Reverend Philip Gaskell, whose earnestness and honesty are not in doubt, but whose mind had not been confused by any study of history. Engels' book opens with the declaration that "the history of the proletariat in England begins with the invention of the steam-engine and of machinery for working cotton." Before their time, he continues,

the workers vegetated throughout a passably comfortable existence, leading a righteous and peaceful life in all piety and probity; and their material condition was far better than that of their successors. They did not need to overwork; they did no more than they chose to do, and yet earned what they needed. They had leisure for healthful work in garden or field, work which, in itself, was recreation for them, and they could take part beside in the recreation and games of their neighbours, and all these games — bowling, cricket, football, etc., contributed to their physical health and vigour. They were, for the most part, strong, well-built people, in whose physique little or no difference from that of their peasant neighbours was discoverable. Their children grew up in fresh country air, and, if they could help their parents at work, it was only occasionally; while of eight or twelve hours work for them there was no question.

It is difficult to say whether this or the lurid picture of the lives of the grandchildren of these people presented in later pages of the book is more completely at variance with the facts. Engels had no doubt whatsoever as to the cause of the deterioration in the condition of labour. "The proletariat," he repeats, "was called into existence by the introduction of machinery." "The

consequences of improvement in machinery under our present social conditions," he asserts, "are, for the working-man, solely injurious, and often in the highest degree oppressive. Every new advance brings with it loss of employment, want and suffering."

Engels has had many disciples, even among those who do not accept the historical materialism of Marx, with which such views are generally connected. Hostility to the machine is associated with hostility to its products and, indeed, to all innovation in consumption. One of the outstanding accomplishments of the new industrial age is to be seen in the greatly increased supply and variety of fabrics offered on the market. Yet the changes in dress are taken as evidence of growing poverty: "The clothing of the working-people in a majority of cases," Engels declares, "is in a very bad condition. The material used for it is not of the best adapted. Wool and linen have almost vanished from the wardrobes of both sexes, and cotton has taken their place. Skirts are made of bleached or coloured cotton goods, and woollen petticoats are rarely to be seen on the wash-line." The truth is that they had never been greatly displayed on the wash line, for woollen goods are liable to shrink. The workers of earlier periods had to make their garments last (second or third hand as many of these were), and soap and water were inimical to the life of clothing. The new, cheap textiles may not have been as hard-wearing as broadcloth, but they were more abundant; and the fact that they could be washed without suffering harm had a bearing, if not on their own life, at least on the lives of those who wore them.

The same hostility is shown to innovation in food and drink. Generations of writers have followed William Cobbett in his hatred of tea. One would have thought that the enormous increase in consumption between the beginning of the eighteenth and the middle of the nineteenth century was one element in a rising standard of comfort; but only a few years ago Professor Parkinson asserted that it was "growing poverty" that made tea increasingly essential to the lower classes as ale was put beyond their means. (This, I may add, unfortunately meant that they were forced to consume sugar, and one must suppose that this practice also led to a fall in the standard of living.) Similarly, Dr. Salaman has recently assured us that the introduction of the potato into the diet of the workers at this time was a factor detrimental to health and that it enabled employers to force down the level of wages — which, it is well known, is always determined by the minimum of food required for subsistence.

Very gradually those who held to these pessimistic views of the effects of industrial change have been forced to yield ground. The painstaking researches of Bowley and Wood have shown that over most of this period, and later, the course of real wages was upward. The proof is not all easy, for it is clear that there were sections of the working classes of whom it was emphatically not true. In the first half of the nineteenth century the population of England was growing, partly because of natural increase, partly as the result of the influx of Irish. For those endowed with little or no skill, marginal productivity, and hence earnings, remained low. A large part of their incomes was spent on commodities (mainly food, drink, and housing), the cost of which had hardly been affected by technical development. That is why so many of the economists, like McCulloch and Mill, were themselves dubious about the beneficial nature of the industrial system. There were, however, large and growing sections of skilled and better-paid workers whose money incomes were rising and who had a substantial margin to spend on the products of the machine, the costs of which were falling progressively. The controversy really rests on which of the groups was increasing most. Generally it is now agreed that for the majority the gain in real wages was substantial.

But this does not dispose of the controversy. Real earnings might have risen, it was said, but it was the quality of life and not the quantity of goods consumed that mattered. In particular, it was the evil conditions of housing and the insanitary conditions of the towns that were called as evidence that the circumstances of labour had worsened. "Everything which here arouses horror and indignation," wrote Engels of Manchester in 1844, "is of recent origin, belongs to the industrial epoch" — and the reader is left to infer that the equally repulsive features of cities like Dublin and Edinburgh, which were scarcely touched by the new industry, were, somehow or other, also the product of the machine.

This is the legend that has spread round the world and has determined the attitude of millions of men and women to labour-saving devices and to those who own them. Indians and Chinese, Egyptians and Negroes, to whose fellow-countrymen today the dwellings of the English of the mid-nineteenth century would be wealth indeed, solemnly declare, in the scripts I have to read, that the English workers were living in conditions unworthy of beasts. They write with indignation about the inefficiency of the sanitation and the absence of civic amenities — the very nature of which is still unknown to the urban workers of a large part of the earth.

Now, no one who has read the reports of the Committee on the Sanitary Condition of the Working Classes of 1842 or that of the Commission on the Health of Towns of 1844 can doubt that the state of affairs was, from the point of view of modern Western civilization, deplorable. But, equally, no one who has read Dorothy George's account of living conditions in London in the eighteenth century can be sure that they had deteriorated. Dr. George herself believes that they had improved, and Clapham declared that the English towns of the mid-century were "less crowded than the great towns of other countries and not, universally, more insanitary." The question I wish to raise, however, is that of responsibility. Engels, as we have seen, attributed the evils to the machine;

others are no less emphatic in attributing them to the Industrial Revolution, which comes to much the same thing. No historian, as far as I know, has looked at the problem through the eyes of those who had the task of building and maintaining the towns.

In the years that followed the long war [1793–1815] the builders had the task of making up arrears of housing and of meeting the needs of a rapidly growing population. They were handicapped by costs, a large part of which arose from fiscal exactions. The expenses of occupying a house were loaded with heavy local burdens, and so the net rent that most workingmen could afford to pay was reduced. In these circumstances, if the relatively poor were to be housed at all, the buildings were bound to be smaller, less substantial, and less well provided with amenities than could be desired. It was emphatically not the machine, not the Industrial Revolution, not even the speculative bricklayer or carpenter that was at fault. Few builders seem to have made fortunes, and the incidence of bankruptcy was high. The fundamental problem was the shortage of houses. Those who blame the jerry-builder remind one of the parson, referred to by Edwin Cannan, who used to upbraid the assembled worshippers for the poor attendance at church.

Stress has rightly been laid by many writers on the inadequacy of the provisions for safeguarding the public against overcrowding of houses on limited sites. But London, Manchester, and other large towns had had their Building Acts for generations, and no one who has looked at the *Builders' Price Books* can possibly believe that Londoners suffered from a deficiency of regulations. Mr. John Summerson, indeed, has suggested that the depressing monotony of the newer streets of the capital were the direct result, not, as is often assumed, of free enterprise, but of the provisions of what the builders called the Black Act of 1774 — a measure that runs to about thirty-five thousand words. It is true that what was uppermost in the minds of those who framed this act was the avoidance of fire. But some writers like the Webbs (as Redford has shown) have done less than justice to the work of the early organs of local government in such matters as the paving, lighting, and cleaning of streets. If more was not done, the fault did not rest on the builders. Thomas Cubitt told the House of Commons that he would not allow a house to be built anywhere unless it could be shown that there was a good drainage and a good way to get rid of water. "I think there should be a public officer paid at the public expense, who should be responsible for that." If the towns were ridden with disease, some at least of the responsibility lay with legislators who, by taxing windows, put a price on light and air and, by taxing bricks and tiles, discouraged the construction of drains and sewers. Those who dwell on the horrors that arose from the fact that the products of the sewers often got mixed up with the drinking water, and attribute this, as all other horrors, to the Industrial Revolution, should be reminded of the obvious fact that without the iron pipe, which was one of the products of that revolution, the problem of enabling people to live a healthy life together in towns could never have been solved.

If my first complaint against commonly accepted views of the economic developments of the nineteenth century is concerned with their pessimism, my second is that they are not informed by any glimmering of economic sense. In the generation of Adam Smith and his immediate successors many treatises appeared dealing with the history of commerce, industry, coinage, public revenue, population, and pauperism. Those who wrote them — men like Anderson, Macpherson, Chalmers, Colquhoun, Lord Liverpool, Sinclair, Eden, Malthus, and Tooke — were either themselves economists or at least were interested in the things that were the concern of Adam Smith, Ricardo, and Mill. There were, it is true, many rebels, on both the right and the left, against the doctrines propounded by the economists; but few of these, it so happened, were historically minded. There was, therefore, no sharply defined cleavage between history and theory. In the second half of the nineteenth century, however, a wide breach appeared. How far it was due to the direct influence of the writings of Marx and Engels, how far to the rise of the Historical School of economists in Germany, and how far to the fact that the English economic historians, following Toynbee, were primarily social reformers, I must not stay to discuss. There can be no doubt, however, that the tendency was to write the story in other than economic terms.

I hold strongly that the future of the subject lies in closer cooperation with the work of economists and that phrases which perhaps served a purpose a generation ago should now be discarded. One of the best historical vindications of American economic civilization has been written, within Sombart's framework, by Professor Hacker. I can only express the opinion that it would have lost little, if any, of its brilliance, and would have been equally convincing, if it had been presented entirely in Professor Hacker's own lucid words. Above all, I do not believe that the centuries have held nothing but cruelty and exploitation. I believe, with George Unwin, that it is from the spontaneous actions and choices of ordinary people that progress — if I may use an anachronistic word — springs and that it is not true that everything rolls on to a predetermined end under the dynamics (whatever that means) of an impersonal force known as capitalism. I believe that the creative achievements of the state have been vastly overrated and that, in the words of Calvin Coolidge, "where the people are the government they do not get rid of their burdens by attempting to unload them on the government." Looking around me, I feel that men are learning by bitter experience the truth of those words. I used to cherish the hope that the study of history might save us from having to learn that way. If I have stressed what seem to me to be the illogical and illiberal tendencies of some of my colleagues, I must end by saying that I am heartened by the knowledge that at the School of Economics and elsewhere in Britain and America there is growing up a body of young teachers who are not antagonistic to economic ways of thought and to liberal ideas. I do not believe that what I regard as the citadels of error will yield to any frontal attack. But I do believe that there are, both in scholarship and in the world of action, forces stirring that give promise of better things.

. . . .

II

The outbreak of hostilities with France in this year [1793] was the occasion of a crisis the essential feature of which (as of all financial crises) was an acute shortage of cash. Fearing for the future, men hoarded their money; merchants were unable to obtain remittances from abroad, or to continue credits to their clients at home; there was a run on the banks, and many houses that were far from insolvent went down for want of coin and notes. The situation was met by a loan from the Government to merchants, in the form of Exchequer bills, and within a short space of time normal dealings were restored. Very soon, however, it was the turn of the Government to be embarrassed by lack of resources. Loans were raised from the public and the proceeds spent, to a large extent overseas. The cost of maintaining the armed forces abroad, and the need to make a loan to the Austrian ally, led to a fall in the rate of exchange. After the disastrous experiment with the *assignats*, France had restored a gold standard, and balances that had been held for safety in London were now being repatriated. So great was the drain of coin and bullion that in 1797 it was necessary to relieve the bank of England of the obligation of meeting its notes in gold. After the suspension of cash payments there was no compulsion on either the Bank itself or the country banks to exercise restraint in the discounting of bills, and so, in time, the volume of the currency expanded, and the level of prices was raised. By 1810 it was plain that sterling had fallen in value in terms not only of goods, but also of foreign currencies and gold. There was much debate then, and there has been more since, as to whether the responsibility for the inflation lay with the Bank of England or the private banks. In fact, it lay with the Government, which by borrowing, and spending the proceeds, raised the money income of the public out of all proportion to the volume of goods available for civilian consumption. Some measure of inflation, it is now generally recognized, is necessary to the conduct of war. If statesmen had followed the advice of Francis Horner and his colleagues of the Bullion Committee of 1810, and had returned to gold at this time, there would have been a fall of prices so great as to put many people out of work and endanger the prosecution of the war. As it was, the rise of prices increased profits, and, since wages limped slowly behind the cost of living, the standard of life of the workers was lowered.

Government borrowing had another, no less important, effect. In 1792, when Britain was at peace, the yield on Consols had been 3.3: five years later it had reached 5.9. Many projects set on foot when money could be obtained at, or near, the first of these rates could not be continued when the cost of borrowing was raised. Capital was deflected from private to public uses, and some of the developments of the industrial revolution were once more brought to a halt. Expenditure on men-of-war, munitions, and uniforms gave a stimulus to ship-building, the manufacture of iron, copper and chemicals, and to some branches of the woollen industry. But the progress of the cotton, hardware, pottery, and other trades suffered a check. In the first phase of the war, building was greatly curtailed, but the peace of 1801–03 brought a revival, and between 1804 and 1815 construction

(though not that of houses) was maintained at a fairly high level.

Foreign trade also suffered less than in earlier wars. After a fall in 1793, exports mounted, with little setback, to a peacetime boom in 1802. The renewal of hostilities was marked by a decline; but for six years the volume of trade was not unsatisfactory, and in 1809–10 there was, once more, a boom. The attempt of Napoleon to bring Britain to her knees by cutting off her markets was a failure. Direct exports to western Europe, indeed, fell away. But the islands of Heligoland and Malta became spearheads by which British trade penetrated to the heart of the Continent, and there was a growth of exports to the West Indies, the United States, and South America. When in 1810, however, Austria was forced to make peace, and Holland was annexed by the French, some of the channels of commerce were closed; and when, in the following year, the Non-Intercourse Act put a stop to trade with the United States, the volume of British exports fell sharply. But the entry of Russia to the conflict in 1812 brought Napoleon's Continental System to an end; and, in spite of the naval war with America, overseas trade remained good in 1813 and 1814 and rose to a peak at the end of the struggle.

Britain had for long offered warehousing facilities for goods in transit from one country to another. During the war it became a major aim of policy to deflect the merchandise of the French West Indies, in particular, to London, and then to re-ship it to Europe and elsewhere. In 1790 about 26 per cent of Britain's exports consisted of goods of foreign origin: by 1800 the percentage was 44, and in 1814 it was still as high as 36. It would be wrong, therefore, to infer that a high level of gross exports meant that all was well with the industries that looked for their markets abroad. The condition of the cotton operatives and nail-makers, in particular, fluctuated with each change in the fortunes of battle and each shift in the tactics of statecraft. But, on the whole, Britain rode through the storm with her people at work: the price of wars for the civilian is paid less when they are in progress than when the fighting has ceased.

In April 1814 Napoleon surrendered his throne and was banished to Elba. For several months British industry was borne on a rising wave of optimism: the rate of interest fell, there was a drop in the price of bread, and both exports and production for home markets were high. But before the end of 1815 the boom had broken. Demobilization threw some 300,000 men on the labour market at a time when industry had not yet adjusted itself to conditions of peace. (The records of the Poor Law are eloquent of the fate of many of these.) European demand for British goods had fallen off, and Government expenditure had been cut by a half. Merchants and industrialists were oppressed by the knowledge that, sooner or later, the monetary standard was to be restored at a parity that could be maintained only if prices were lowered. Private investment was at an ebb and unemployment was widespread. Poor harvests in 1816 and 1817 caused food prices to rise and the demand for manufactured goods to fall. In 1818, indeed, conditions improved. Low rates of interest, revived Government expenditure, better harvests, livelier markets abroad, and a raised level of construction at home brought a brief boom. But the three following years were less favoured; and it was not until 1821 that the era of inactive capital and unemployed labour — the era of what we now call reconversion and deflation — was brought to an end.

The experiences of these years have clouded for many the true nature of the technical and economic changes of the period. Just as the war had thwarted the purpose, so the conditions in which peace was restored postponed the fulfilment of the revolution in industry. There was, there can be no doubt, alongside the distress, a growth of class feeling and bitterness. Much of this arose, less from a conflict between capital and labour, than from an opposition of views as to where the burden of increased taxation should lie. A Parliament representative largely of landlords demanded the repeal of the income tax, which had been imposed as a war measure, and the introduction of increased duties on grain. It was submitted, not without reason, that the agricultural classes already bore, through the land tax, the tithes, and the poor rates, the greater part of the cost of the public and ecclesiastical establishments. And it was urged, with less justice, that the political services which the landowners rendered entitled them to special consideration from the State. The Corn Law of 1815, which prohibited the release to the millers of wheat from abroad so long as the price at home was below 80 shillings a quarter, was intended to preserve for the agriculturists a structure of prices and rents that had been created by war — at a time when manufacturers were being forced to sell their products more cheaply, and when money wages tended to fall. In fact, the domestic price of wheat rarely reached 80 shillings. The defect of the law was not that it maintained a consistently high level of prices for grain, but that, in times of dearth, it prohibited relief from abroad until conditions approached those of famine.

Apart from this fiscal injustice, the workers had grounds for complaint. Some, instructed by Tom Paine and William Cobbett, resented their lack of political status, and many had learnt by experience of the limits the law of combination imposed on their bargaining strength. Throughout the eighteenth century, riots had been endemic: again and again the pitmen and sailors, shipwrights and dockers, and the journeymen of the varied trades of London downed tools, smashed windows, and burnt effigies of those with whom they were at variance. About many such incidents there had been something of the lightheartedness of the May Day demonstration. But the tumults of the second decade of the nineteenth century sounded a deeper and more disturbing note. Those who took part in them were not, in the main, factory operatives, but workers who belonged to the older system of industry: the croppers of Yorkshire, the frame-work knitters of Nottingham, and the hand-loom weavers of Lancashire. Under-employed and under-fed men were not over-nice in theorizing as to the cause of their distress, and it was natural enough that they should strike at the machines that appeared to be taking the bread from their mouths. Some of the unemployment was, indeed, the result of technical change; but the chronology of revolt points to the real cause of the trouble. It was in 1811, and again in 1816, when political events and bad harvests had led to depression, that the Luddites destroyed the stocking-frames in the Midlands and the power-looms in the North. It was in 1817 that the hungry and workless Blanketeers set off on their dismal march from Ardwick Green. And it was in 1819, when, once again, bread was scarce and trade at low ebb, that the working-class Reformers of Lancashire gathered, and suffered, at St. Peter's Field. The story of repression — of the Home Office spies and the ill-famed Six Acts — has been told too often to bear repetition here. Frightened politicians and an inept administration were not the least of the misfortunes of these unhappy years.

In the early 'twenties many circumstances combined to produce high prosperity. The currency was established on a foundation of gold and there was a run of favourable harvests. Huskisson and his colleagues were active in pulling down tariffs, lowering excise duties, and removing restrictions from industry and trade: the policy of reform by repeal was good in the eyes of men who had been irked by controls and who asked only to be let alone. A substantial part of the National Debt was converted from 5 to 4 or 3½ per cent: in 1820 the yield on Consols had been 4.4; by 1824 it was 3.3. In 1822 Bank rate, which had stood for almost half a century at 5, was brought down to 4. But Bank rate was not yet a mirror of market conditions, and in the early months of 1825 short-term loans were being placed at little more than 2½ per cent. In Lancashire and Scotland factories were run up at unprecedented speed, and between 1821 and 1825 the output of bricks more than doubled. Ironworks were busy producing piping for gas and water undertakings and sections for bridges and railways. Stocks of cotton, wool, and other raw materials were built up. Overseas trade expanded; and, since re-exports now constituted only 16 or 17 per cent of the goods sent abroad, the growth was almost entirely the outcome of increased productivity of industry. Canning's recognition of the emancipated colonies of Spain, in 1823, gave a fillip to foreign investment: Latin America seemed to offer boundless opportunities for trade, and the export of capital to this area played a large part in the boom.

High expectations of profit led to a burst of speculative schemes in 1825: many of these were bogus, and others, inherently sound, failed to yield returns as fully, or as promptly, as had been hoped. Since incomes and prices had risen, the exchanges took a downward turn, and there was an almost simultaneous internal and external drain of gold. Correctives were applied. Interest rates were raised and credit was contracted: prices fell and unemployment became widespread. It is unnecessary to detail the story of the depression of 1826, the recovery of 1827, the prosperity of 1828, and the gloom and agricultural distress of 1829 and 1830. The cyclones and anticyclones of the 'twenties were of the same nature as those that were to pass over England many times in the later decades of the nineteenth century.

It was through such changing seas that the captains of the industrial revolution steered their courses. Many of the difficulties they encountered were, it is clear, of their own making. Some of the navigators were unable to distinguish a false wind from a true, and not all knew when it was safe to clap on sail, or prudent to shorten it. Not all, again, took sufficient thought of the state of their crews: pioneers have often suffered disaster by reason of this. But the major troubles arose, not from want of skill or want of heart — certainly not from want of courage — but from the forces of Nature and the currents of political change. If harvests had been uniformly good; if statesmen had directed their attention to providing a stable standard of value and a proper medium of exchange; if there had been no wars to force up prices, raise rates of interest, and turn resources to destruction, the course of the industrial revolution would have been smoother, and its consequences would not have been, as they are, in dispute.

Some of these consequences, it must be admitted, were baleful. In spite of the efforts of Thomas Percival and James Watt, the skies over Manchester and Birmingham grew dark with smoke, and life in the cities became drab. The smaller industrial town, like Oldham or Bilston, had a harsh countenance: towns, to be good, should grow slowly. There was, it seems likely, a decline of taste — as the very letterpress of the books to which the student goes for his data bears witness. But all was not loss. The face of England is patient of modulation: enclosing landlords and planters gave it new grace. Nor were the early industrialists insensitive to the appeal of the country: the beauty of Cromford and Millers Dale suffered little by the enterprise of Arkwright, and stretches of the Goyt and the Bollin owe something to Oldknow and the Gregs. Even the products of manufacture are not to be thought of as wholly uncomely: Telford's Anglesey bridge and the pottery of Wedgwood and Spode cry out against that. If large-scale industry overshadowed art and craftsmanship, it did not by any means destroy them.

Much has been written about the effects of the industrial revolution on the workers. Some, impressed by the lot of those who went down in the struggle against the machine, have declared that technological change brought little but misery and poverty, and a statistician of repute has set on record his opinion that by the early years

of the nineteenth century the standard of life of the British worker had been forced down to Asiatic levels. Mr. Colin Clark can hardly have looked at the statistics which more than a generation of research has produced. The careful studies of Mrs. Gilboy indicate that, over the eighteenth century, the material well-being of the labourer in the woollen area of the South-West had, indeed, fallen, but that the lot of his fellow in the textile region of the North had steadily improved, and that the labourer of London more than held his own. It is true that the rise of prices after 1793 made many humble people poorer. But before the end of the war (as Professor Silberling has shown) industrial wages in England caught up with retail prices, and in the 'twenties the gain was pronounced. In 1831 the cost of living was 11 per cent higher than in 1790, but over this span of time urban wages had increased, it appears, by no less than 43 per cent.

It would have been strange, indeed, if the industrial revolution had simply made the rich richer and the poor poorer. For the commodities to which it gave rise were not, in general, luxuries, but necessaries and capital goods. The tardiness with which the last of these yielded their fruit to the consumer has already been explained. But by the 'twenties the effects of the war were passing away and the cottons and woollens, and food and drink, which now became available, were consumed not by the few, but by the masses. Some of the products of the factories and ironworks were sent abroad, but the return cargoes did not consist, in the main, of wines and silks, but of sugar, grain, coffee, and tea for the people at large. Much has been made of the suggestion that the prices of the things Britain exported fell more rapidly than those of the things she brought back: there was no revolution to reduce costs in overseas agriculture; and British lending abroad may also have helped to give the terms of trade an unfavourable turn. But, though such influences may explain why, in the 'thirties and 'forties, real wages were lower than might have been expected, they had little effect, it would seem, between 1815 and 1830. The diet of the worker almost certainly improved: there was a substitution of 'flower of wheat' for rye and oatmeal; and meat, which had been a rarity, became, with potatoes, the staple dish on the artisan's table. Not all the coal raised from the pits went to feed the furnaces and steam-engines: a warm hearth and a hot meal were of no small consequence to the man who came home wet from the fields.

In 1802 George Chalmers remarked that the laborious classes were "too wealthy to covet the pittance of the soldier, or too independent to court the dangers of the sailor." There were, true enough, many vagrants and paupers, but, even before the new Poor Law came in, the hordes of the "indigent and distressed" had probably shrunk. Hours of labour were long, and holidays few; there is a mass of evidence that employment in factories was harmful to the health and morals of the young. A leading politician has recently spoken of the "mechanized horrors of the industrial revolution," and there can be little doubt that the deeper mines and more complicated machines brought new risks of mutilation and death. But against all this must be set the lessening of the strain on those who worked in the heavy trades, and the decline in the number of crippled and deformed people that followed the introduction of power in places like Sheffield. There must be set, also, the reduction of sweating of women and young children, the rise in family earnings, the greater regularity of pay, and the gain in welfare that came as industrial work was taken out of the home.

Whether the houses themselves were becoming better or worse is difficult to determine: much depends on the periods compared. Many of the dwellings provided for the workers by the country factory master have survived — at Cromford, Mellor, and Styal. They have design and proportion, are not wanting in amenity and comfort. But these were put up when building materials were plentiful, wages

relatively low, and money relatively cheap. After 1793 the import of timber from the Baltic was restricted, and the price of labour of bricklayers and carpenters went up. At least two-thirds of the rent of a dwelling consists of interest charges: rates of interest were rising, and for more than a generation they remained high. This meant that if dwellings were to be let at rents which the workers could afford to pay they had to be smaller and less durable than those of the 'eighties. The rows of ill-built, back-to-back houses, into which the rapidly growing population of the towns was pressed, were largely the product of wartime conditions.

After 1815 matters were made worse by the influx of Irish, who, gregarious by instinct, crowded into the seaports and the towns of the North. Careful estimates made by members of the Manchester Statistical Society in the middle 'thirties led to the conclusion that about one-sixth of the families in Manchester were Irish, and that the percentage of the people living in cellars was 11.75. In Liverpool, where again there were many Irish, no less than 15 per cent of the inhabitants were in cellars. But in the newer towns, which were the special creation of the industrial revolution, conditions were far less grim. In Bury, where there were few Irish (and few hand-loom weavers) only 3.75 per cent, and in Ashton-under-Lyne only 1.25 per cent of the people were housed in this way. In these places, the investigators reported, the houses of the workers were not only less crowded, but also better furnished and cleaner than those of the cities.

An historian has written of "the disasters of the industrial revolution." If by this he means that the years 1760–1830 were darkened by wars and made cheerless by dearth, no objection can be made to the phrase. But if he means that the technical and economic changes were themselves the source of calamity the opinion is surely perverse. The central problem of the age was how to feed and clothe and employ generations of children outnumbering by far those of any earlier time. Ireland was faced by the same problem. Failing to solve it, she lost in the 'forties about a fifth of her people by emigration or starvation and disease. If England had remained a nation of cultivators and craftsmen, she could hardly have escaped the same fate, and, at best, the weight of a growing population must have pressed down the spring of her spirit. She was delivered, not by her rulers, but by those who, seeking no doubt their own narrow ends, had the wit and resource to devise new instruments of production and new methods of administering industry. There are to-day on the plains of India and China men and women, plague-ridden and hungry, living lives little better, to outward appearance, than those of the cattle that toil with them by day and share their places of sleep by night. Such Asiatic standards, and such unmechanized horrors, are the lot of those who increase their numbers without passing through an industrial revolution.

THE TRADE CYCLE, LIVING STANDARDS, AND MOVEMENTS OF DISCONTENT

WALT WHITMAN ROSTOW

Professor at Massachusetts Institute of Technology, Rostow has spent several years at Oxford, and his major work has been done on nineteenth century Britain, especially, with Gayer and Schwartz, *Growth and Fluctuation of the British Economy, 1790–1850* (2 vols., 1953). The essay here printed is among the least technical of his writings. It illustrates his interest in demonstrating the connection between economic growth (with emphasis on its statistical measurement) and social and political movements.

Historians of every shade of bias admit the importance of the influence of economic situations on political and social events. The weight attached to economic factors or, more precisely, the mechanism of their action is, however, by no means settled. The most familiar relation that has hitherto been emphasized in the years 1790–1850 links the mechanical inventions of the late eighteenth century to the growth of the factory system and to the consequent rise of a large urban proletariat and a powerful middle class. From these relations, which are essentially sociological, efforts have been made to explain the political forces that produced the Reform Bill of 1832, the Chartist Movement, the repeal of the Corn Laws. In the realm of cultural history, the rise to dominance of a philosophy of individualism and a cult of romanticism have been linked to the same forces, with ramifications in economic doctrine, religion, architecture, and poetry. Such attempts at interconnexion represent a long-run analysis of economic influences. For many purposes, especially where economic influences operate at several removes, that sort of generalization is adequate.

Experience of the inter-war years, however, impressed observers with the tremendous impact of economic forces, acting over shorter periods. Changes in social structure, in political atmosphere and policy, and in intellectual attitudes can be more or less directly traced to the depression after 1929. While it is true that these trends (and the causes of depression as well) have a long history reaching back, at least, to 1873, their timing, their intensity, and their unique character are closely connected with recent short-run developments. Many historians have taken account of this type of influence, but rarely have they done so systematically.

From 1790 to 1850 there were at least three major economic forces that contributed, at intervals, to British social and political unrest: cyclical unemployment, fluctuations in domestic harvests, and technological unemployment. The latter, by itself, was not likely to produce major disturbances; nor can it be sharply distin-

From Walt Whitman Rostow, *British Economy of the Nineteenth Century*, (Oxford, 1948). Chapter 5, pp. 108–22. By permission of the Clarendon Press.

guished from cyclical unemployment. The underemployment of hand-loom weavers was, admittedly, an important element in the Luddite and Chartist movements; and the resentment of the hand-loom weavers against the introduction of machinery often gave a peculiar character to the activity of wider groups. The most serious unrest, however, was a product of cyclical depression and high food prices.

Good harvests with resulting low grain prices were calculated to call forth complaint from the landholders and from tenants burdened with fixed rent payments. The demand for grain was sufficiently inelastic to bring a decline in gross income when good harvests caused a sharp fall in price; and, until 1832 at least, the agrarian interest was disproportionately represented in Parliament. The simplest short-period, economic-political relation is that between the wheat price and the Corn Laws.

The Corn Laws were altered principally in the following years: 1791, 1804, 1815, 1822, 1828, 1842. Repeal came, of course, in 1846. A glance at the annual average wheat price reveals the principal setting for these amendments.

The wheat price fell from 56 shillings per quarter in May 1790 to 42s. in October 1791. The movement continued to a low point of 47.0s. in May 1792. The harvest of 1791 was "one of great abundance" and, under the prevailing corn law, the fall in price was sufficient to cause the ports to be closed to foreign grain: "but the low price was productive, as usual, of complaint on the part of the landed interest, and was the occasion of a fresh corn bill." The inadequate harvests of the following years, however, kept the wheat price at or above 50s., and the Act of 1791 was not called into operation.

The catastrophic fall in the wheat price, from 154s. per quarter in March 1801 to 50s. in February 1804, produced similar, though even more violent complaint. The Corn Laws were again modified. The area under cultivation had, of course, been greatly expanded between 1793 and 1804.

A succession of abundant harvests brought forth an unparalleled supply of wheat. The import limit was raised to 63s. The cutting off of Baltic supplies resulting from the resumption of war, together with bad harvests, kept the wheat price above the new minimum until 1815. Like the Act of 1791, that of 1804 was never operative.

From August 1812, when the wheat price was 152s., to January 1816 a steady decline took place. The break-up of the continental system and finally, the return to peace, as well as good harvests, caused this fall. Despite considerable opposition it was judged that only an 80s. import limit could protect the capital newly invested in agriculture.

Until the close of 1818 the wheat price remained above 80s., aided largely by inadequate harvests on the Continent and considerable exports from Britain to France. But good harvests then brought on a decline to 39s. at the close of 1822. The period of severe agricultural distress has coloured the whole view of British agriculture in the three decades after the Napoleonic wars. In 1822, however, the Government was trapped between the farmers' petitions and the opposition to further protection from labour, commercial, and industrial interests. At Peterloo, three years before, "No Corn Laws" had appeared on the banners. Unlike the position in 1815 the decline in agricultural prices (1818–22) was accompanied by a decline in import prices and non-agricultural domestic prices. The Corn Law of 1822 modified only slightly the terms of the Act of 1815. "The farmers had asked for bread and gotten a stone"; but there were others, too, asking for bread between 1818 and 1822.

From the second quarter of 1823 to the last quarter of 1828 the price of wheat hovered between 50s. and 70s. per quarter. Although the farmers were far from content, their relative position was, with respect to profits, probably no worse than that of the manufacturer or exporter; after the crisis of 1825, in fact, it was probably better. And those who sought a reduction in agricultural protection were victorious in the Corn Law of 1828. It is probable that the growing prestige of free-trade ideas and the parliamentary influence of industrial and mercantile groups played some part in moderating the 1815 bill. There was however, an immediate economic basis reflected crudely in the movement of relative prices in the twenties:

	Domestic price index	Import price index	Wheat price (s. per quarter)
1823	97	99	52
1827	106	82	56

It is clear that, from 1823 to 1827, the wheat price did not share the net fall experienced in most other markets. After 1825, a peak year in general prosperity, this disparity was especially felt; and it was in the post-crisis atmosphere that antagonism to the Corn Law of 1815 developed.

Until the last quarter of 1832 the wheat price remained well above 50s. and, although the farmers never ceased to complain, their position was not desperate. The three following years (1833–6), however, brought abundant harvests, low prices, and extensive parliamentary investigations. Although the pressure for further protection increased, no action was taken by a Parliament in which anti-agrarian interests had been materially strengthened by the Reform Bill of 1832.

At the close of 1836 the wheat price again rose suddenly as the harvest of that year appeared inadequate. Chronically bad yields kept the price abnormally high until 1842. In this period the anti-Corn Law forces crystallized outside of Parliament, deriving additional strength from the generally depressed state of industry and the high level of unemployment, especially after 1839. This protracted pressure on real wages helped bring about the Whig tariff reforms of 1841: but "Corn duties they left where they were, crying over their shoulders as they were being pushed out of office that a reasonable fixed duty . . . was the right thing." Peel was elected on the issue

of the sliding scale, and in 1842 his modifications of the Corn Law of 1828 consisted in lowering the maximum duty and in making the sliding scale less steep. He himself believed this arrangement to be a considerable reduction in protection, and it was put forward as such. There is no doubt that the high food prices and depression in the previous few years had, by 1842, helped to discredit the whole argument for agricultural protection and for tariffs generally.

The role of the Irish famine in the suspension and, ultimately, in the repeal of the Corn Laws is a familiar short-period sequence, as is also the tangled and dramatic political story of 1846. It is probable, in fact, that strictly economic considerations played a somewhat lesser part in the final repeal than in some of the earlier modifications. In 1845 and the first three quarters of 1846 the domestic wheat price ranged between 45s. and 59s. A few years before it had been over 70s. The Irish famine might have been dealt with by extraordinary measures short of actual repeal. The rise in the wheat price (to a peak of 93s. in June) in 1847, however, would almost certainly have ended agricultural protection then, if its end had not been accomplished earlier.

This account is not meant, of course, to deny the long-period factors making for a reduction in agricultural protection: the growth of population, the accelerated industrialization of Britain, the widening political power of the urban middle classes and their free-trade doctrines. But it is clear that the timing of the events leading up to repeal were closely connected with the British harvests and other short-run factors influencing the absolute and relative level of the prices of agricultural products.

1. *The Speenhamland System, 1795.* The years 1794 and 1795 saw some industrial recovery in Great Britain, from the depression of 1793. A more powerful force, however, affecting labour's position, was a rise in foodstuff prices, due primarily to bad harvests. The wheat price was 43.2s. per quarter in January 1792, 108s. in Au-

gust 1795. Although money wages rose, there seems little doubt that they rose "in a very inadequate proportion to the increased price of the necessaries of life." There was widespread evidence of physical distress, and the wage-subsidy scheme for out-of-door relief was instituted, much in the tradition of the Elizabethan poor laws.

2. *The Combination Acts, 1799 and 1800.* From the last quarter of 1796 until about the middle of 1799 the price of wheat and the cost of living remained moderately low. Despite the brief but severe depression of 1797, these were, internally, years of relative peace. The wheat price (which, at the end of 1798, was down to 48s.) then rose to a peak of 154s. in March 1801. The government acted by offering bounties on grain imports, by sending agents to the Baltic ports, and by encouraging the process of inclosure. In 1799–1801, in general, the working classes were fairly well employed. Even the crisis in the Hamburg trade, in 1799, did not induce a prolonged deflation. Under these circumstances the workers had considerable market leverage in contracting money-wage bargains. In the attempt to maintain their real wage, at a time of rapidly rising costs of living, the men resorted to various types of combination. Even agricultural workers banded together in certain areas, notably in Norfolk.

Although the combination movement was very much the outgrowth of a particular short-period situation, and although the typical expression of discontent was the local bread riot or strike, the unrest was, at times, successfully linked with republican ideas. The corresponding societies, particularly, attempted to shape and unify the general dissatisfaction around the current liberal platform. With the memory of the French Revolution in mind, the Government acted to repress the corresponding societies and the combinations. The Acts of 1799 and 1800, reinforcing existing legislation, made illegal all collective working-class activity except the guild functions of the friendly societies.

3. *The Repeal of the Combination Acts,*

1824 and 1825. From 1820 through the early months of 1825 a fairly continuous increase in output and employment occurred. In the latter stages of the boom prices rose, relieving manufacturers briefly from the chronic downward pressure that had existed since 1814. But the period 1820–4 saw a coincidence of increased output and a sagging price level. Foodstuff prices, too, were fairly low. It is not surprising, then, that in the four years after Peterloo British labour was relatively peaceful.

The fact of increased prosperity, too, made it possible for the industrialists and the Government to afford a greater tolerance. Exceptional measures of repression were allowed gradually to lapse; the activities of spies were relaxed; and the law was set less freely in motion against working-class attempts at combination. It was in this atmosphere, early in 1824, that Place and Hume manoeuvred the repeal of the Combination Acts.

The repeal immediately brought into the open the trade unions which had been operating under cover in the previous two decades; and it encouraged the formation of many others. A wave of strikes broke out and, in the following year, an aroused Parliament seriously limited the easy-going terms of the Act of 1824.

There can be little doubt that the strikes of 1824–5 can, in some measure, be attributed to the repeal of the Combination Acts. Two other factors, however, were operating. In the first place, in the latter half of 1824, the boom was suddenly accelerated, pushing the major British industries close to full employment. Enormous exports to South America and to the United States, as well as widespread internal enterprise, created a typical, late prosperity situation. Strikes for higher wages would normally be expected.

This tendency was accentuated by a second factor, a sudden rise in living costs.

In 1825, with a confidence born of some five years of increasing employment, the unions instituted numerous strikes for higher wages — in the cotton, wool, coal, iron, building, and other trades. At about the middle of 1825, however, the business cycle turned downward; and, although the strikes continued for some time, by the end of the year "combination . . . was knocked on the head. Bradford weavers and combers went back to work at the old wages . . . so did Renfrewshire colliers." In the bitter industrial conflicts that continued into 1826, labour was no longer on the offensive, but attempting to preserve wage rates in the face of a declining industrial demand.

The repeal of the Combination Acts is properly regarded as an expression of the general trend toward *laissez-faire,* paralleled, in the twenties, by the Huskisson tariff reforms. Hume, in Parliament, presented the measure in such a light. Both Hume and Place regarded the unions as illiberal institutions brought into being by the repressive action of the Government; and they looked forward to their disappearance with the repeal of the Combination Acts. Nevertheless, the tolerant action of Parliament in 1824 was directly connected with the previous years of prosperity; the violence of the strikes of 1824–5 was largely the outgrowth of the situation in the labour market on either side of the cyclical turning-point, accentuated by the rising costs of living. It is possible, too, that the intemperance of the reaction of the Government in withdrawing, in 1825, a large part of the freedom granted in the previous year, may be linked to the change in the industrial outlook which occurred in that year. With commodity prices falling, and disillusion setting in with respect to the newly floated Latin-American mining issues, the doctrine of *laissez-faire,* as applied to labour organization, seemed somewhat more empty than in 1824.

4. *The Factory Act of 1847.* Factory acts in the first half of the nineteenth century were passed in 1802, 1819, 1833, 1842, and 1847. Each arose in a unique political setting; but each saw a similar combination of humanitarian and anti-industrial groups arrayed against the manufacturers. Within the ranks of the manufacturers there were, of course, notable exceptions: men like Peel and Whitbread and Owen, to whom the conditions of factory labour were ethically outrageous and/or who believed that shorter hours and better conditions meant greater efficiency and profits. In parliamentary debate, humanitarian arguments led to rebuttal based on pleas for the freedom of the individual, or originating in attacks on state paternalism. To these the manufacturers would often add the claim that shorter hours meant a serious reduction or even the destruction of the existing margin of profit, and the loss of foreign markets.

There is, however, probably some significance in the fact that these acts were all passed at, or close to, a low point in cyclical fluctuations. The years 1819 and 1842 are such troughs in general business conditions, while 1833 and 1847 were also generally depressed years (the troughs were in 1832 and 1848). To a limited extent the children and women working in factories and mines were competing with the men available for the jobs. At a time of severe cyclical unemployment it would be natural, then, that the men should complain, and attempt to oust their competitors or to limit their working time. A major driving force behind the movement which led to the Act of 1833, for example, was "the hope of absorbing men who are 'hanging on the trade idle.' "

In the case of the Ten-hour Bill of 1847 the role of the depression is even more clear. From 1845 onward unemployment was steadily increasing. In 1844 a Ten-hour Bill was defeated; in 1847 it was quietly passed. *The Times,* in a leading article on the following day, said it was not to be imagined that there had been any considerable degree of conversion on the subject. The argument stood very much where it had done in 1844, and had, in fact, been almost exhausted in that memorable struggle. The absence of fierce opposition was attributed in a large measure to the fact that the chief argument of the opponents — namely, that the country could not spare the last two hours of industry — could not be brought forward in 1847 without inviting its own refutation, for so great was the depression of trade that the mill owners found it impossible to keep their mills working for so long as ten hours.

From the side of the workers, too, a distinctly non-humanitarian factor can be detected in the ten-hour agitation. There seems to be little question that the labour unions viewed the measure as a means of restricting the labour supply and maintaining wage rates at a time of serious depression. At an early stage of the ten-hour agitation (December 1841) in a period of severe unemployment, Fielden was reported to have said: "It is the duty of individuals to curtail the quantity of production when there is an over-abundant supply of the article they produce rather than increase it and reduce wages. He considered that a reduction of the hours of labour from twelve to ten would have this tendency, and was therefore desirable, as they had already got mills and machinery to produce more than they could find a vent for at a remunerating price."

To some extent, then, the Ten-hour Bill was passed because unemployment existed and because it was believed by some to be a recovery measure. In markets other than that for labour the restriction of supply, in an effort to maintain prices, was a typical depression phenomenon in these years.

The long-run economic and social influences reflected in the debates are perhaps more familiar. In Parliament, the factory question, from this time down to 1847, was really a part of the wider struggle between the agricultural landlords and the manufacturers over the repeal of the Corn Laws. The Tories were taunted with the condition of the labourers in the fields, and they retorted by tales of the conditions of the operatives in factories. The manufacturers rejoined by asking, if they were so anxious to benefit the workman, why did they not, by repealing the Corn Laws, cheapen his bread. The landlords and the mill owners

each reproached the other with exercising the virtues of humanity at other people's expense. This is not to deny, of course, that sincere humanitarians worked within the Ten-hour Movement; nor does it underrate the importance of the strange political battle which led, finally, to the passage of the 1847 Bill. But it is clearly a case where the short-run position of the economic system — the degree of unemployment — played a part in determining the moment of its ultimate acceptance.

Testifying before the Committee on Manufactures (1832) William Mathews, Staffordshire iron manufacturer, was asked: "9991. Do you conceive that the depression of trade in late years has had any effect in producing . . . discontent? — Very great. 9992. Do you think the working classes of Staffordshire ever show political discontent so long as they are doing well in their particular trade? — Not at all; you cannot get them to talk of politics so long as they are well employed. 9993. Do you think that any man could create discontent among them so long as they were doing well? — It is utterly impossible." The converse of the dictum — "you cannot get them to talk of politics as long as they are well employed" — is not to be generalized without reservation; but within this period it serves to explain the political unrest of such years as 1811–12, 1816, 1819, 1826, 1837, 1839–42, and 1847–8. In each of these cases a fairly direct connexion can be traced between unemployment and mass dissatisfaction. In the case of the Reform Bill, for example, to which Mathews's questioners were referring, there can be little doubt that the intense depression of the latter months of 1831 and the early months of 1832 contributed significantly to the pressures that led to its passage.

The activities of the Chartists, covering more than a decade, offer an interesting, if somewhat crude confirmation of this thesis. General business conditions reached a peak in 1836; 1837 was a year of severe depression; some recovery followed through 1838, to a second peak early in 1839. From the later months of 1839 to the end of 1842 Britain suffered almost unbroken depression, exacerbated in its effects on the working classes by bad harvests. A recovery set in during 1843 which culminated in a peak in 1845. Business activity then declined to a low point in 1848. The phases of the most important Chartist activity occurred within severe depression; its temporary, but almost complete disappearance in 1843–5 coincides with the prosperity of those years.

The three focal points of Chartist activity came in 1839, 1842, and 1848. Beginning in 1837 the Movement gradually grew to the point where a petition boasting some million and a quarter signatures was presented to Parliament in 1839. The failure of this petition, and the Government's prosecution of the leaders, caused a temporary stagnation; but in 1842 a petition containing almost three and a third million names was placed in the hands of the Government. In that year, too, the Chartists helped lead a series of bitter strikes, marked by extensive sabotage.

The wheat price fell, with the advent of a promising harvest, in the summer of 1842, and in the following year recovery was well under way. For the Chartists a long period of discouragement and inactivity followed, until the return of depression in 1846. Still another petition went to Parliament in that year, and throughout 1847 the strength of the movement increased. Early in 1848 there were large meetings in the principal cities, climaxed by the presentation of the signatures of what purported to be almost six million British men and women. Threats of direct action, however, failed to materialize, and, in the following years, prosperity and inadequate leadership brought the movement to an end.

The demand for universal suffrage at this period in British history patently had roots deeper than cyclical unemployment. The chronically depressed position of the hand-loom weavers, many of whom were Chartists, was also more than a cyclical problem. Yet, apparently, depression was required before the political doctrines of the Chartist leaders could command wide or effective support.

These examples by no means exhaust the possibility of tracing important links between short-run economic fluctuations and political and social events in the years 1790–1850. There are innumerable other cases which might usefully be examined from this perspective, and those traced here deserve more detailed analysis. Even these brief summaries, however, reveal the manner in which cyclical fluctuations and cost-of-living movements served to detonate and to give expression to the familiar underlying trends. They should also emphasize the distinctive economic, social, and political atmosphere of each year, or even different parts of the same year. The use of long-run conceptions like "the growth of the Free-trade Movement," or the "development of working-class organizations," or "the Industrial Revolution" tends to blur this type of distinction. A necessary, but by no means sufficient requirement for a thorough inter-relation of economic and other factors is a knowledge of fluctuations in general business activity and in costs of living.

THE DESTRUCTION OF THE
PEASANT VILLAGE

PAUL MANTOUX

Born in 1877, Paul Mantoux gained his reputation as an economic historian by writing, in 1906, the book from which the following excerpt is taken. Although he held several academic appointments after 1906, he has published no other major work, and much of his career between the wars was spent in quite different ways, in particular as interpreter at the Peace Conference of 1919, and then in the Secretariat of the League of Nations. The view here stated has long been the most widely accepted judgment on the agrarian side of eighteenth century economic change.

THERE WAS one obstacle in the way of the new methods. It was the existence of the open fields. For the greater part, those "unenclosed fields" were very badly cultivated: the arable lands, in spite of fallow years, were exhausted by the monotonous alternation of the same crops — the pastures, left to themselves, were overgrown with heather and gorse. How could it have been otherwise? Each farmer was tied down to the common rules. The system of crop rotation adopted for the whole parish was only suitable for some of the lands, and the other lands suffered thereby. The cattle and sheep fed on weeds, and their promiscuous mixing together was the cause of murrains. As for improvements, any man who attempted them would have ruined himself. He could not drain his fields without the consent and concurrence of his many neighbours. Each plot was contained within fixed limits and was too narrow to admit of cross-harrowing, as recommended by Jethro Tull. Before a farmer could choose his own time for sowing, the custom of allowing the open field to be used as a common grazing ground for several months in every year had first to be abolished. No such thing could be contemplated as growing an unwonted crop, or sowing clover where there had been rye or barley. To all these disadvantages should be added the extraordinary complication of the system, and the endless quarrels and lawsuits that were its inevitable consequence. In the olden days, when farming had been a traditional calling, an accepted inheritance that supported a man year in year out, such a state of things could be put up with. But to the modern farmer, who looks upon agriculture as a business undertaking and reckons up exactly his expense and profits, the compulsory waste on the one hand, and, on the other, the sheer impossibility of doing anything whatever to increase the produce, are simply intolerable. The open-field system was doomed, therefore, to disappear.

Between the sixteenth- and seventeenth-century enclosures and those of the eighteenth century, there was an essential difference. The former had been opposed by the

From Paul Mantoux, *The Industrial Revolution of the Eighteenth Century*, English Translation, (London, 1928), Part I, Chapter 3, pp. 168–80, 181–90. By permission of Jonathan Cape Limited.

King's administration, the latter, on the contrary, met with assistance and encouragement from Parliament. Under the Tudors and Stuarts, enclosure was either the result of sheer spoliation, or of a mutual agreement between all the landowners of a parish. But the mighty had means at their disposal to suppress any opposition: "Unwilling commoners are threatened with the risks of long and expensive lawsuits; in other cases they are subject to persecution by the great proprietors who ditch in their own demesne and force them to go a long way round to their own land, or maliciously breed rabbits and keep geese on adjoining ground, to the detriment of their crops." Once enrolled in Chancery, the agreements could be enforced without any further formality. In the eighteenth century, the method was further improved. Whenever it was found impossible to obtain the necessary assent for concluding a *deed of mutual agreement,* the legal authorities could step in. All the Acts of Enclosure on the Statute Book, without exception, are evidence of so many cases when the unanimous consent of the landowners could not be secured. But no legal action could be taken unless there was a request for it. Here we shall see on whose initiative and for whose profit the enclosures were made.

The great landowners were the first to undertake a methodical exploitation of their estates according to the precepts of the new agricultural science. They were the men who bore most impatiently the obligations laid on them by the open-field system. And they, in almost every case, initiated the petition to Parliament for a Bill of Enclosure. As a rule, they began by holding a conference and choosing an attorney who was to be in charge of the legal side of the proceedings. The next step was to call a general meeting of all the landowners. In that meeting, the decision was not reached by a majority of individual votes: the importance of each voter was proportionate to the acreage of his land. For the petition to be considered in order, the number of signatories was of small account: but they must represent four-fifths of the lands to be enclosed. Those who owned the last fifth were often fairly numerous, sometimes they were the majority. Some petitions bore two or three names only, some could be found bearing but a single name. True, they were important, impressive names, accompanied by titles which recommended them to the considerate attention of Parliament. If the consent of some small landowner was indispensable, he was asked for it in such a manner that he could scarcely refuse. The local grandees — the lord of the manor, the vicar, the country squires — laid the request before him in tones which, we may surmise, resembled a command rather than an entreaty. If the man resisted, he was threatened, and he gave his signature even though he might withdraw it later. But very few occasions arose for taking such action; the villagers scarcely dared show their discontent: what they feared above all things was to "appear against their superiors."

Once the petition was duly signed, it was brought before Parliament. Then began a series of expensive proceedings of which the wealthier landowners bore the cost. Parliament was all for them: did not their own mandatories, their friends and relatives, sit in the House? The heads of the ancient nobility in the House of Lords, as also the many country squires in the House of Commons, were the representatives of the great landed interests. It often happened that the Bill was drafted at once, without any preliminary inquiry. When an inquiry was ordered, its conclusions were almost invariably identical with the desires of the petitioners. Counter-petitions had results in one case only, namely when they too originated in the possessing and ruling classes. The claims of the lord of the manor, who would suffer no curtailment of his former rights, those of the vicar, who wanted compensation for his tithes, had every chance of being received favourably. Where a single man owned one-fifth of the acreage to be enclosed, his opposition was enough to put an end to the proceedings.

Thus, what the great landowners had done, could be undone by the great landowners alone.

What happened after the Bill of Enclosure had been passed? Although it was as a rule a lengthy document, burdened with complicated clauses, it did no more than prescribe the general conditions of the operation: on the spot only, and in the presence of the parties concerned, could points of details be settled. A considerable and most delicate task remained then to be fulfilled. It consisted in actually finding out what was the state of every property, measuring all the plots of land that went to make it up, reckoning the income it brought in, as well as the relative value of the rights of common enjoyed by each owner. It was necessary to consider the whole territory of the parish, the common field together with the open field, to cut it into portions equivalent to the scattered properties for which they were to be substituted; to grant compensation, if the case arose, to direct and supervise the setting up of the fences that were now to divide one man's land from his neighbours'; to see that undertakings in the common interest prescribed by the Act, such as road-making or mending, drainage, irrigation, were duly carried out. In fact, all this was tantamount to a revolution throughout the parish — the land being, so to speak, seized and dealt out again among the landowners in an entirely new manner, which, however, was to leave untouched the former rights of each of them. To ensure that this division should be carried out equitably, that errors and arbitrary measures should be avoided, what minute care, what a fine sense of valuation, and also what impartiality, what detachment from private interest, would have been required!

That very important and delicate task was entrusted to commissioners, to the number of three, five or seven. As far as the enclosure was concerned, they exercised unrestricted authority. In the words of Arthur Young, "they are a sort of despotic monarch, into whose hands the property of the parish is invested, to re-cast and re-distribute it at their pleasure." For a long time, there was no appeal from their decisions. It is most interesting, therefore, to know who these commissioners were, what social class they came from, by whom they were appointed. In theory, they held their authority from Parliament: their names were in the Act of Enclosure. But, since Parliament took no interest in and had no knowledge of the local questions that the commissioners were to settle, they were in fact nominated by the petitioners: which means that their appointment, even as all the previous proceedings, was in the hands of the great landowners. Here once more, the same characters played the foremost parts: "the lord of the soil, the rector and a few of the principal commoners monopolize and distribute the appointments." They chose men devoted to them, unless they preferred to sit on the Commission themselves. The unlimited authority of the commissioners was no other than their own. It is not very surprising that they should have used it to their own advantage.

The abuse was so plain that the most determined supporters of enclosures, and those least likely to oppose the interests of the great landowners, denounced it emphatically. In 1770, Arthur Young put forward a request, that the commissioners be elected in a meeting of all the landowners, and be made responsible to the county magistrates. But his protest did not secure attention, and not until 1801 — when a general Bill was enacted for the purpose of settling once and for all the clauses common to all Acts of Enclosure — were any steps taken to prevent the inflicting of grievous wrongs. It was forbidden to appoint as commissioners the lord of the manor, his stewards, bailiffs or agents either in his service, or having left it less than three years before, or "any proprietor or person immediately interested in such moors, common or waste lands, half-year lands or uninclosed lands, intended to be . . . inclosed." Henceforward, the commissioners were under the obligation of giving a hearing to all complaints and mentioning them in their reports. Any person with a grievance had a right to appeal from the commissioners' decision to the Quarter Sessions. This belated legislation is evidence of spoliations that had been committed and had remained unpunished for a century.

The small man, whose field was not a capital to him, but a bare means of living, could but look on helplessly while those changes took place, and his right to his land, together with the very conditions of his existence, were in question. He could not prevent the commissioners reserving the best lands for richer men. He was constrained to accept the lot assigned for him, even though he might not consider it an equivalent of his former property. He lost his rights on the common, which was now to be divided. A portion of that common land was indeed allotted to him; but its size was in proportion to the number of animals he used to graze on the lord's waste. Thus, once more, he that had most, received most. Once in possession of his new land, the yeoman had to fence it round, and this cost him both labour and money. He had to pay his share of the expense incurred in carrying out the Act — and those expenses were often very heavy. He could not fail to be left poorer than before, if not actually burdened with debt.

As for the cottager who was traditionally allowed to live on the common, gather his firewood there, and perhaps keep a milch-cow, all that he considered as his possession was taken away from him at a blow. Nor had he any right to complain, for after all, the common was the property of other men. The possessing classes were unanimous in thinking that "the argument of robbing the poor was fallacious. *They had no legal title to the common land.*" This was so, no doubt, but they had until then enjoyed the advantages of a *de facto* situation, sanctioned by long tradition. Some writers have maintained that these advantages amounted to very little and that their loss could not seriously injure the cottagers. The law, however, seems to have recognized the grievous wrong inflicted on them: an Act

of Parliament, passed in 1757, directed the commissioners for enclosures to pay into the hands of the Poor Law authorities certain compensations "to be applied towards the relief of the poor in the parish or township where . . . wastes, woods and pastures had been enclosed." This implied a recognition of the fact that the dividing up of the common was the cause of hardships. A further step was sometimes taken to alleviate them: a piece of ground was kept undivided for the use of the poorer inhabitants of the parish, the landless cottagers, or else they were awarded small lots whereon to graze their wretched flocks. But such compensation was seldom granted, and was in any case illusory: the lots were so very small and inadequate that the cottagers seized the first opportunity to dispose of them and make a little money. Nor had they long to wait.

For, after the enclosure had been made, the shares allotted, the fences set up around each piece of land, all was not yet over. The great landowners had not yet reaped all the profit they expected from the operation. After consolidating their estates, they sought to increase them, and, when nothing remained to be taken, they were prepared to buy. Some wished to add to their ploughed fields and meadows; others wanted to enlarge their parks or their hunting grounds; others yet, in a few cases, would "buy cottages near their mansions, for no other purpose than to shut them up, and to let them decay, because they did not like to have the poor for their neighbours." And besides those who were already great landowners, others — merchants, bankers, and later, manufacturers — longed to rank with them. The moment was a favourable one. The redistribution of property had caused a wavering among the class that was most closely, most devotedly attached to the soil. The honest, hard-working, but shortsighted yeoman, a follower of the beaten track, was bewildered by the changes around him, and felt a coming danger in the formidable competition of the great farms run on modern methods. Whether he became dis-

couraged or chose to seek his fortunes elsewhere, he was tempted by the rich man's
offers, and sold his land.

Almost everywhere, the enclosing of
open fields and the division of common
land were followed by the sale of a great
many properties. The enclosures and the
engrossing of farms are two facts which
eighteenth-century writers considered as inseparable, whether they wished to speak for
or against them. The engrossing of farms
was not always a consequence of the enclosure; sometimes, on the contrary, it took
place before an enclosure. But whether it
was the consequence or the purpose of the
operation, we know for certain that the
total number of farms had become very
much smaller in the latter half of the century. One village in Dorsetshire where, in
1780, as many as thirty farms could be
found, fifteen years later had the whole of
its land divided between two holdings; in
one parish in Hertfordshire, three landowners had together engrossed no less than
twenty-four farms, with acreages averaging
between 50 and 150 acres. An admirer of
enclosures, little inclined to exaggerate
their evil effects, put the number of small
farms absorbed into larger ones between
1740 and 1788 as an average of four or five
in each parish, which brings the total to
forty or fifty thousand for the whole Kingdom. Here was the important fact, un-
doubtedly more important than the division
of the commons, although it disturbed the
public opinion of the time much less. It
was carried out by means of private deeds,
unobtrusively and without any intervention either by Parliament or the local authorities; and it almost escaped notice. But
it was the real end towards which efforts of
the great landowners were ultimately directed; the enclosures and all their array of
legal proceedings were chiefly the means of
compelling the farmers to sell their land,
or of improving estates that had been en-
larged by recent purchases. The figure of
forty to fifty thousand farms in less than
fifty years, which does not seem exaggerated, shows how far-reaching were the

changes wrought in landed property in the
course of that half-century.

It is true that the disappearance of a
farm did not necessarily mean that of a
property. Engrossing often consisted in
joining together several small holdings on
an estate into one larger farm. But that
very change amounted to a revolution, for
it involved deep modifications in the
method of cultivation and in the use of
labour.

During the first two-thirds of the eighteenth century, the reduction in the number
of small holdings was followed, as in the
days of the Tudors, by the extension of pasture land. Arthur Young, in his *Farmer's
Letters* (1767), wrote that a farm could
make better profits by breeding than by
tillage, and cost less labour. A number of
counties where cultivation still held its
ground, in spite of previous enclosures,
now put on a new aspect. Towards the end
of the century, Leicestershire, that had
been famous for its crops, was almost entirely covered with artificial meadows; more
than one-half of Derbyshire, three-quarters
of Cheshire, three-quarters of Lancashire,
had become grazing land. Since 1765 or so,
the rise in prices stimulated corn-growing,
and the movement for transforming tilled
land into pasture slackened down. But even
if the cultivation of oats or wheat required
more labour than the rearing of sheep, the
total number of farm-hands had, in any
case, been reduced. Was it not one of the
chief aims of the joining together of the
plots formerly scattered over the open fields,
to effect such a reduction?

The Bills of Enclosure met with little
active opposition; nor is the reason far to
seek. Those who had most to complain of
dared scarcely lift their voices. If they ven-
tured to put forth a claim or send a petition
to Parliament, the only probable result for
them was money spent fruitlessly — legal
expenses, or the fees of experts, counsels
and solicitors. Often they would merely
refuse to sign the petition drafted by their
neighbours, the great landowners: even
then, they would at once declare that they

did not mean to oppose that petition: an attitude showing that the villager, as the phrase goes, "knew his betters." Thus, formal protests were comparatively rare. Yet a few of them have reached us. Sometimes they attacked the very principle of the enclosure, as being "very injurious to the petitioners, and tending to the ruin of many, especially the poorer"; sometimes they denounced its operation as "partial and unjust . . . hurtful to the petitioners in particular and to the community in general." After 1760, such protests became more frequent and forceful. The suppressed anger of the villagers would break out suddenly. In some parishes, the announcement of the enclosure caused riots. Formal notices could not be posted on the church doors, because of the obstruction by riotous mobs, who forcibly prevented the sticking up of bills. The constable in charge of those bills was confronted by threatening crowds, armed with cudgels and pitchforks: in a Suffolk village, on three successive Sundays, his notices were torn out of his hands, he was thrown into a ditch, and stones were hurled at him.

This passionate opposition, in strong contrast with the villagers' habitual timorousness, may have had no other cause than an instinctive distrust of change. But we find it supported by a full array of documents and facts. According to these, the enclosures resulted in the buying up of the land by the wealthier class; they lay at the root of all the evils of the period — the high cost of necessaries, the demoralization of the lower classes and the aggravation of poverty. "It is no uncommon thing for four or five wealthy graziers to engross a large inclosed lordship, which was before in the hands of twenty or thirty farmers, and as many smaller tenants or proprietors. All these are thereby thrown out of their livings, and many other families, who were chiefly employed and supported by them, such as blacksmiths, carpenters, wheelwrights and other artificers and tradesmen, besides their own labourers and servants." Not only had the small landowner to give

up his land, and either to leave the district or fall to the condition of labourer, not only was the cottager evicted from the common, but as the large farms needed comparatively less labour, a number of journeymen were left unemployed.

The result was depopulation, if not everywhere, at least in a number of rural districts.

The enclosures also had admirers who dwelt upon their undeniable advantages, and strove to prove that most of the evil consequences imputed to them were purely imaginary. The most earnest among them were the writers on husbandry, in whose eyes the distribution of the land had far less importance than its capacity for production. For them the supreme argument was that large holdings offered the best conditions for the practical and theoretical progress of agriculture. Arthur Young compared big farms to big workshops, and, after quoting Adam Smith's famous passage on the manufacture of pins, he added: "Agriculture will not admit of this, for men cannot be employed their whole lives in sowing, others in ploughing, others in hedging, others in hoeing, and so on, but the nearer we approach to this the better: which can only be on a large farm. In a small one, the same man is shepherd, hogherd, cowherd, ploughman, and sower; he goes about ten different sorts of labour and attention in the same day, and consequently acquires no habitual skill peculiar to himself." Yeoman farms were ill-cultivated, and "generally the residence of poverty and misery." The great landowner had more intelligence and initiative, and above all he could afford to make experiments and undertake more or less expensive improvements. Wherever enclosure had taken place and large farms had been established, there had been a rise in rent. This was an unanswerable argument for those students of agriculture, who were at the same time economists, and to whom men were of little account when production and profit were at stake.

They could hardly dispute the fact that

the consolidation of estates very often resulted in the absorption of small holdings, but they denied that the condition of labourers had become worse in consequence. We know what their opinion was concerning the division of common lands; arguments against it, they thought, were "grounded on mistaken principles of humanity." As for complaints about the reduced demand for agricultural labour and the depopulation of villages, they dismissed them as absurd stories. How could anyone believe that to let part of the land lie fallow and to cultivate the rest as badly as possible was the means to occupy and feed the greatest possible number of men? "This appears to my poor understanding a most extraordinary paradox. There is in my neighbourhood a fine heath, consisting of about a thousand acres. In its present uncultivated state, it does not support a single family, nor does almost anyone receive benefit from it, but some of the farmers around, who occasionally turn a few of their cattle upon it. Whereas, were it enclosed, well cultivated and improved, it would make six or eight good farms, from £70 to £100 a year each. These, besides the farmers and their several households, would require near thirty labourers, who, together with their wives and children, added to the tradesmen and mechanics that would be necessary to supply their respective wants, would raise the population on this single spot, in the course of a very few years, at least two hundred persons." To make such optimistic calculations more likely, carefully selected figures were brought forward, showing that the ill effects of engrossing were more than compensated by the cultivation of the waste lands. It was even maintained that cultivation on a large scale was the system that would give the rural population the best opportunities in respect of both work and wages. At the same time, those who represented the body of opinion hostile to enclosures were committing an error and supplying their adversaries with a ready argument. They believed that, all over the Kingdom, the population was de-

creasing, and they represented the alarming fact as a consequence of the enclosures. The party of the agricultural experts had no difficulty in proving that this alleged depopulation of England was a mere fancy and whenever, on the contrary, they observed an increase in the population of any county, they did not fail to attribute it to the beneficial changes in the distribution of the land. Their triumph was easier still when, as disciples of Adam Smith, they adopted the economic point of view: a system that resulted in the production of the largest quantity of goods at the smallest cost must be the best system for the whole community. If this is not admitted, they said, the Turks rightly object to the introduction of the printing press, which might be prejudicial to the copying profession, "and all civilized Europe is in error." Would any one be so ill-advised as to maintain that the husbandman should lay by the plough and take up the spade to dig the earth, on the plea that this would afford labour for a larger number of men?

Yet they made some significant admissions. In spite of their optimism, they bore witness to the wrongs suffered by the poor under their very eyes. A commissioner of enclosures wrote: "I lament that I have been accessory to injuring two thousand poor people at the rate of twenty families per parish. Numbers, in the practice of feeding on the commons, cannot prove their right; and many, indeed most who have allotments, have not more than one acre, which being insufficient for the man's cow, both cow and land are usually sold to the opulent farmers." After an impartial inquiry, the Board of Agriculture acknowledged that in most cases the poor had been stripped of what little they owned. In some villages, they could not even get milk for their children. The available evidence is heart-rending in its monotony. The Earl of Leicester, upon being congratulated on his newly-built castle at Holkham, answered with remorseful melancholy: "It is a sad thing for a man to be alone in the district of his residence: I look around, and can see no other house than mine. I am like the ogre in the tale, and have eaten up all my neighbours."

Does this mean that those neighbours had disappeared, that they had been wiped out like a nation overrun by barbarous hordes? No, indeed. But a section of the rural population, having been torn away from the land that nourished them, having lost their homes and seen their former ties broken, became unsettled and migratory; the small landowners and farmers on the one hand, the cottagers and journeymen on the other, were ready to leave the countryside if they could make a better, or indeed a plain, living elsewhere.

Let us consider these two classes of men in turn. One is no other than the smaller yeomanry, whose decline will now be comprehensible. There was no room for them in the system which had been framed by the apostles of the new agriculture and carried out by means of Acts of Enclosure: Arthur Young asked what would be the use to a modern State of having a whole province cultivated by peasant proprietors, as in the early days of Rome, "except for the mere purpose of breeding men, which of itself is a most useless purpose." On the large estates, the exploitation of which was methodically conducted by their wealthy owners, a new type of farmer made his appearance, who compares with the old-time farmer as a millowner compares with the master manufacturer. He paid a high rent and looked forward to high profits, and the sort of life he was able to lead would have been regarded as extravagant by a country squire of the previous generation. He fed well, and, when he had friends to dinner, offered them claret or port wine. His daughter was taught to play the harpsichord and dressed "like the daughter of a duke." There was nothing in common between him and the labourer in his employment, and he was very unlike the old yeoman whose place he had taken, although he often sprang from the yeomanry. But, for one small landowner who succeeded in exchanging his former independence for the position of a prosperous tenant, how many were driven either to work as hired labourers, or to leave their villages?

The temptation to go in search of work was still greater for unemployed labourers. In many localities the men in need of parochial relief were sent round from one farm to another for employment, part of their wages being paid from the poor rates. They formed thus a somewhat unsettled element, and were ready to go anywhere to find occupation, whenever they succeeded in evading the servitude imposed on them by the Poor Law, which bound the pauper to his parish. This, according to the supporters of the new system of agriculture, explained the seeming depopulation of the country, which was used as an argument against enclosures. "The men were not lost but, perhaps, with the ground, better employed." If there was less time and labour wasted on the land it was for the benefit of the towns and of their trades. Before 1760 a movement of population could already be observed "from rural parishes to market towns, and from both of them to the capital city: so that great multitudes of people who were born in rural parishes are continually acquiring settlements in cities or towns, particularly in those towns where considerable manufactures are carried on." Industry was in fact the only refuge for thousands of men who found themselves cut off from their traditional occupations. The manufacturers were to offer them the living they could no longer earn on the land.

On the movement of rural labour in search of work information is scanty and unreliable. But whenever such information can be obtained, it reveals the steady movement of land-workers to industrial towns. "About forty years ago [this was written in 1794] the southern and eastern parts of the county (Warwick) consisted mostly of open fields, which are now chiefly inclosed... Upon all inclosures of open fields the farms have generally been made much larger. These lands being now grazed want much fewer hands to manage them than they did in their former open state: from these causes the hardy yeomanry in country villages have been driven for employment into Birmingham, Coventry and other manufacturing towns." A petition signed by the inhabitants of a rural parish of Northamptonshire describes the local peasantry as "driven from necessity and want of employ, in vast crowds, into manufacturing towns, where the very nature of their employment, over the loom or the forge, may waste their strength, and in consequence debilitate their posterity."

Thus the enclosures and the engrossing of farms resulted in placing at the disposal of industry resources in labour and energy which made it possible for the factory system to develop. Industry was becoming, as it were, a new land in the very midst of the country, another America attracting immigrants by the thousand — with this difference: that instead of being a discovery it was a creation, the very existence of this new world being conditioned by the increase of population. Each newcomer brought with him what he had been able to save before leaving the old country. Those among the yeomen who had suffered least from the redistribution of the land, and had succeeded in getting a fair price for their property, were in possession of a small capital. Having, more or less against their own will, given up their rooted traditions and habits, they were now ready to try their fortune in the new field by launching into ventures which on all sides attracted their enterprise. From their number were to rise many of the first generation of manufacturers, who started and led the industrial movement, and were soon to form a class of men rivalling in wealth and influence the great landowners now in possession of their land. But comparatively few, of course, attained that degree of success. Many of the small yeomen and farmers, reduced to the condition of wage-earners, shared the fate of the labourers who came to the towns in search of work. They possessed nothing, and could offer nothing, but their labour. They were to form the working population, the anonymous multitude in the factories — the army of the industrial revolution.

The changes in the conditions of rural life had a still more direct influence on the progress of industry. We know that one of the characteristic features of the domestic system of manufacture was the scattering of workshops in the villages, the very basis of that system consisting in a close alliance between cottage industry and the cultivation of small holdings. We have noticed how a weaver would eke out his earnings with the product of a plot of ground, and how a rural family would in the evening spin wool for the merchant manufacturer. The blow dealt to peasant property broke that time-honoured alliance of labour on the land and industrial work. The village artisan, when deprived of his field and of his rights of common, could not continue to work at home. He was forced to give up whatever independence he still seemed to have retained, and had to accept the wages offered to him in the employer's workshop. Thus labour was becoming more and more concentrated, even before the competition of machinery had finally destroyed the old village industries.

There is, therefore, an intimate connection between the movement by which English agriculture was transformed, and the rise of the factory system. The connection being of a less simple nature than a mere relation between cause and effect, the two events might at first sight appear to have sprung from entirely different sources, only influencing each other in the course of their respective developments. The disappearance of the yeomanry, for instance, was not caused by the industrial revolution, but the industrial revolution made it more rapid and complete. As for the movement of labour from country to town, it certainly assisted, though it could not have determined, the progress of industry. If one of the two factors had been lacking, would not the other have continued to develop, although most probably its progress would have taken a somewhat different course?

Had the bulk of the rural population remained on the land, the triumph of the factory system might have come later, but it could not have been indefinitely postponed, as is shown conclusively by what took place in France. Might it not therefore be held that the relation between the transformation of agriculture and that of industry was limited to accidental influences — technical improvements based on entirely different methods accounting in both cases for separate and parallel developments?

But these improvements, independent though their progress may seem to be, were only part of a more general evolution, and their success was largely due to the support they received from each other. The growth of great industrial centres would have been impossible if agricultural production had not been so organized as to provide for the needs of a large industrial population, and agricultural production, on the other hand, could not have developed had not the industrial districts supplied adequate markets with growing numbers of consumers. This was one of the favourite arguments used by the advocates of enclosure: "By the produce being greater there will be a surplus for manufactures, and by this means manufactures, one of the mines of the nation, will increase in proportion to the quantity of corn produced." And, while the two movements were thus connected in their respective consequences, another and stronger connection was that between their causes. What accounts for the change in rural conditions, for the enclosures, the division of the common lands and the engrossing of farms, is the introduction of a business spirit into the management of agriculture, landowners thereafter considering the land as capital, from which a better income could be drawn by improved methods of exploitation. In agriculture, as in industry, the initiative of the capitalist proved both self-seeking and beneficial to the community, for it did away at the same time with obnoxious routine and with old institutions, to which the working men were still looking for protection. The conditions of all successful business are the reduction of cost and the increase of profit. The enclosures resulted in a reduction of labour and an increase of production. A comparison between their effect and that of the introduction of machinery was well justified, for their ultimate origin was one and the same.

ENCLOSURES AND THE RURAL
POPULATION: A Revision

JONATHAN D. CHAMBERS

J. D. Chambers teaches at the University of Nottingham. By comparison with some of the writers represented in this book, he has published little. But he has been a leader in the application of modern scholarly methods to the study of local and regional history, especially that of the East Midlands of England. The article here printed is not easy to read. But it is a first-class example of the work of local historians of the present generation, showing as it does both the kinds of material they use and the type of reasoning which, they think, should supplement the more sweeping generalizations of those who study whole countries and continents.

Since writing this article, Dr. Chambers has made further enquiries into the question on the basis of the burial and baptism records. The results will be found in his *The Vale of Trent 1670–1800: A Regional Study of Economic Change* (Cambridge, 1957). They show that the period 1720–50 was marked by years of very heavy mortality, especially the years 1727–9, when large numbers of children died as a result of epidemics brought on, perhaps, by bad weather and short harvests. Recovery from this setback was checked by the bad years of 1736, 1741, 1748–9, with the result that the death rate, especially of children, was high in spite of low prices. After 1750 the evidence suggests that the death rate began to fall, and in spite of setbacks it continued to fall until the end of the century. At the same time food prices were rising; thus it would appear that the low prices of 1730 did not cause a fall in the infant death rate, while a rise in prices after 1750 did not prevent a fall in the death rate. Dr. Chambers thinks that part of the explanation may be that the virulence of epidemics was greater before 1750 than afterwards, though he can offer no reason for this. Perhaps also the environmental changes, such as better clothes, food and houses, were already at work, though the evidence for this is not easy to find. Whatever the reason, the result would be that the lower age-groups would become more numerous; this would serve as a stimulus to economic expansion both on the side of an increase in the supply of labour—especially child labour—and of demand for food, houses, and the products of industry. The expanding economic opportunities, he suggests, stimulated early marriage, and the size of families in the industrial areas appears to have risen. Thus there was a falling death rate alongside a very high birth rate; but the causes are still under discussion and the last word has not been said.

The passage is taken from Jonathan D. Chambers, "Enclosures and Labour Supply in the Industrial Revolution," *The Economic History Review*, Second Series, V, No. 3 (1953), pp. 319–24, 325–8, 331–4, 335–6, 337–43. By permission of the author and *The Economic History Review*.

UNTIL the advance, a generation ago, in the study of the demographic aspect of the Industrial Revolution, the function of enclosure in regard to labour supply was regarded as crucial. Its special importance in recruiting the industrial labour force was developed in a series of important studies as the result of which it came to be generally regarded as a basic postulate of the new large-scale economy. More recent examination of the growth and movement of population has done something to modify this view, but the conventional picture of catastrophic change effected by enclosure continues to find adherents. Any alternative to it, says Mr. Maurice Dobb (*Studies in the Development of Capitalism,* 1947), implies the assumption that "the appearance of a reserve army of labour was a simple product of growing population which created more hands than could be fed from the then cultivated soil. If this were the true story, one might have reason to speak of a proletariat as a natural rather than an institutional creation and to treat accumulation of capital and the growth of a proletariat as autonomous and independent processes. But this idyllic picture fails to accord with the facts." This formulation of the problem invites discussion on several counts, but from the angle of the regional historian (from which it is viewed here) it generalizes a process which he sees in terms of its separate parts, i.e. as actual movements of population in particular places; and he is impelled by the force of his methodology to test the abstract formula of "institutional creation" by fitting it to the local facts as he knows them. Such is the purpose of this article; but some clarification of the formula is necessary at the outset.

The question which is raised here is not the institutional origin of the proletariat, but whether enclosure is the relevant institution; not whether the growth of the proletariat can be treated in isolation from capital accumulation, but what form the relationship took. It centres on the emergence of what Professor Tawney (*The Agrarian Problem in the Sixteenth Century,* 1912) has called "a residual population" of propertyless free labour, and the factors, in addition to enclosure and eviction, which accounted for its growth; and a brief résumé of the early stages of the problem is necessary to indicate the context of its later stages with which we are here concerned. It is relevant, for instance, to recall that as early as the thirteenth century, among the limiting conditions for the growth of a free labour force, were the localized customs of partible and impartible inheritance and the influence they exerted on the age of marriage. In the area of open-field or "Champion" England, where, we are told, holdings usually descended undivided to one son, the rise of a free labour force from younger sons and daughters would have taken place more rapidly but for customary restraints upon their marriage. These, it has been suggested, would be relaxed when alternative means, e.g. the domestic woollen industry, were offered for rearing a family. Here was a potential source of labour power that could be expected to respond to the stimulus of investment all the more freely for the absence of the counter-attraction of partible inheritance.

These sources of growth operated silently and perhaps we may say organically, i.e. they were not the direct or indirect product of compulsion; and for that reason there is a danger that they may be overlooked. For opposite reasons enclosure and eviction may be given too much importance: they operated, in Mr. Dobb's phrase, "institutionally," i.e. compulsorily, as the result of the exercise of power, and stirred the social conscience to protest and the victims to riot and rebellion. But their effectiveness as a recruiting agent for the labour army remains a doubtful quantity, especially in the light of the knowledge we now have of the scale on which they worked. Sixty villages "wiped out," fifty of them by enclosure between 1450–1600 in Leicestershire alone; the desertion of ninety-three sites in Warwickshire and "other hundreds yet to be discovered": changes of this order must have made a sizeable contribution to the army of the landless; but it seems to have provided only a temporary alleviation of the labour shortage and did little to stimulate population growth. "The problem of population," says Professor Tawney, "was the problem of under-population"; and contemporary writers were beginning to explore the possibilities of rewards for parents of large families and penalties for bachelors.

The period immediately preceding the era of parliamentary enclosure with which we are primarily concerned here, seems to have followed a not dissimilar pattern; it was marked by the buying out of freeholds and leases for lives as a prelude to enclosure on such a scale as to give rise to the erroneous view that the yeomanry had already disappeared by 1750. But rapid and ruthless as this process may have been, it failed to meet the labour needs of the time or to accelerate substantially the processes of proletarian reproduction. "The fear of scarcity of labour," we are told, "seems constantly in the minds of eighteenth-century employers"; and "for a century following the Restoration," says Mr. Dobb, "the growth of capitalist industry must have been considerably handicapped by the comparative weakness of the labour army"; but, from the middle of the eighteenth century, "the pace of dispossession quickens"; and enclosure at last takes place on a scale sufficient to perform its allotted task of reducing the peasantry to a landless proletariat and removing the last prudential checks upon their increase.

At this point, the existence of census returns, enclosure awards and land tax duplicates makes possible the application of more exact tests to the claims which are made for enclosure in recruiting the labour force, and to this aspect of the discussion we may now turn.

The first effect of bringing this method of quantitative inquiry to bear on the problem seems to be to diminish the role assigned to enclosure. Professor Gonner, in his exhaustive study of census returns, could find no general connexion between enclosure and movement of population. Professor Redford finds that the impact of agricultural change at least during the war years was more often to stimulate the growth of rural population than the reverse, and that side by side with the growth of urban communities, there was also a growth of entirely new agricultural communities as well as the reinforcement of those already existing. Among the examples he gives we might refer especially to Lincolnshire, where the distressing lack of originality in rural nomenclature emphasises the novelty of the new creations: East Ville, Midville, West Ville, Langcrick Ville, to mention only four entirely new communities emerging as a result of the enclosure act of 1812. There was a parallel movement in Cheshire where the enclosure of Delamere Forest was the midwife of a new community. And the enclosures of Sherwood Forest, Charnwood, Enfield Chase, Bere Forest, Beeley Heath, Hampton Common, of wastes in Cumberland, Dorset, Derbyshire, Lancashire, Yorkshire, Northumberland, continued to stimulate the growth of population in rural areas almost up to the middle of the century.

But it may be objected that the peopling of the waste places is merely a variant in a rural setting of the movement of expropriated peasants from the old established rural centres under the expulsive force of enclosure. It is also possible that such a movement was masked by the growth of rural industries, and that the extruded peasantry were being transformed into a rural industrial proletariat as the first step to their recruitment in the army of urban labour.

An attempt has been made to examine this objection within a limited area of 119 villages in Nottinghamshire. It shows that the population of the predominantly agricultural villages rose only less fast than that of the villages in which manufacturing or mining industry prevailed; and that of the agricultural villages, those that had been enclosed by act of parliament before 1800, rose faster than any.

Such evidence, however, leaves the larger

question unanswered. The increase in population which is seen to be taking place in all types of village, whether enclosed or not, may well be compatible with the reduction of the small-scale producer to the level of labourer and a stripping of the cottagers of their last remaining vestiges of independence. In regard to the section loosely called the yeomanry, that is (to adopt the working definition of Sir John Clapham) the farmer-owner with a holding sufficient to occupy his whole time, it would appear that he held his own or even made something of a recovery, at least during the war-time boom, and that the post-war decline was not catastrophic, as the Agricultural Reports of 1833 and 1836 show.

In regard to the earlier period when it is suggested the yeomanry actually made something of a recovery, we need make no more than a passing reference to the many examples quoted by the Agricultural Reporters to show that economic conditions were not always unfavourable to the independent owner-occupier and that there was a widespread tendency to buy on the rising market. Where the soil was favourable to the small freeholder, enclosure might permit him to develop a form of mixed husbandry, as in South Wiltshire, where "there are so many parts of the land, that, when enclosed, may be applied to the purposes of a small farm, without the necessity of keeping a flock of sheep to manure it; viz. by keeping that part which will be necessary to maintain in arable, on a turnip system . . . by laying the wet parts to grass . . . and by applying the sand lands on a garden system."

Most of these examples refer to the small owner. The small tenant was in a far worse case and contemporary opinion leaves us in no doubt that this class generally suffered in numbers heavily from enclosure; but the economic context of enclosure cannot be assumed always to have been fatal to the small man at this time; it varied in its incidence according to local circumstances. Enclosure marked only a phase — though an important one — in the ascendancy of

the large farm with its lower comparative costs; it was not the signal for the extinction of the small farm as an economic unit everywhere.

If we turn to the statistical evidence, we find confirmation of this supposition. A number of localized inquiries may be cited which tend to show that the survival-value of the small man under the impact of enclosure should not be underestimated. In Professor Lavrovsky's exhaustive analysis of eleven villages in Suffolk enclosed between 1797 and 1814 he finds that the peasantry, in the form of small owners and leaseholders, were very numerous before enclosure, and that the former were somewhat more numerous afterwards. Moreover, owners and tenants were so intertwined that it was difficult to distinguish between them, as they frequently held land from each other besides occupying their own, and a surprisingly large number were absentee landowners. After enclosure, the copyholders as well as the freeholders received allotments in compensation for the loss of common rights; common-right owners without land were compensated and so came into the category of landowners for the first time, thus increasing the numbers of the smallest owners, i.e. the cottagers with an average just under ten acres each. But in size of properties the average amount held by the smallest owners remained unchanged while that of the handful of larger owners was substantially increased, the effect of enclosure thus being to accentuate the economic differentiation between large and small owners while adding to the numerical advantage of the latter. In a further study of twenty enclosure awards in different parts of the country he finds there were few large farms but (except in four out of the twenty) a numerous peasantry. Moreover, the awards indicate, he says, "an extraordinary development of peasant ownership" as a result of the sale and division of some of the large farms; and he refers especially to the village of Newbold in Leicestershire, where at the auction of land held by the Commissioners to defray expenses, nineteen small owners, who he thinks were new to the parish as their names were not found among those receiving allotments at the enclosure, acquired an average of three acres each. Whether the small tenants came off equally well is another matter. As Professor Lavrovsky says, they were more immediately affected "as parliamentary enclosure signified the temporary suspension and annulment of leases, though it is true on a basis of some 'compensation' to lessees." There may have been consolidation and a reduction in numbers; "doubtless, large farms might have been formed under favourable circumstances," to quote this scrupulously careful author again, but the fact that so many of the tenants were also small owners would serve as a brake upon any catastrophic fall into the category of landless labourers.

Nothing, however, is said of the lowest group of all, the cottage labourers with customary usage of the common; and nothing statistically can be said. Since they had no proprietory rights to defend they do not appear in the enclosure award or land-tax returns though they occasionally occur in estate accounts, as in the case of the Duke of Kingston's accounts of Gedling, Carlton and Stoke Bardolph where sixteen cottagers paid rent before enclosure but none afterwards; these landless or semi-landless workers, together with the small tenants who disappeared through consolidation, represent the real victims of enclosure, and unless they are constantly kept in mind, they may also become the victims of the statistical method. It is of such — tenant cottagers and small tenant farmers — that Dr. Hasbach can truthfully say: "Enclosure was the last act in the drama of proletarianization"; but it does not seem that this was necessarily true of the smallest owner or copyholder who could substantiate a legal claim to the satisfaction of the enclosure commissioners; and in the light of recent research it would seem that the commissioners were not too difficult to satisfy. Indeed, they stand in striking and pleasing contrast to the squires and rich yeomen of the fifteenth and sixteenth centuries who "wiped out" the villages of the Midlands by the hundred, turning the dispossessed away "tearfully" and "into idleness." Whatever may be said of the method of enclosure by act of parliament, it represents a milestone in the recognition of the *legal* rights of humble men.

So much for the immediate effects of enclosure in these thirty-six examples examined by Professor Lavrovsky. What of the delayed effects — the fencing of allotments and paying the expenses of enclosure? Unfortunately, no answer can be given to this question for the villages under review, and in order to throw light on it the results of inquiries elsewhere must be explored. There is for instance the interesting study — the most extensive yet made — by Mr. Swales of seventy Parliamentary enclosures in Lindsey in which he finds that the number of owners receiving allotments reached a total of 1,374 of whom 82 per cent were owners of less than 50 acres. The burden of expenses was heavy on the small owners and he cites between seventy and eighty examples of sales in nine villages either before or after enclosure. There may have been more of which he has no knowledge, and there is evidence, in the case of the earliest examples, of substantial decline after enclosure; but the author has no doubt from the evidence of the land tax returns that this loss was more than made up afterwards by the influx of fresh purchasers during the period of high prices, especially in the Fen parishes.

Elsewhere, in Lincolnshire, the small owner, wherever economic conditions favoured him, was very strong, whether subject to enclosure or not; Arthur Young, writing in 1799, notices 146 proprietors at Kirton Laceby, apparently a village of old enclosure, "where every man lives of his own"; in the Fens where half the area was in the hands of small freeholders. The Lincolnshire historian Canon Massingberd was certainly correct when he said, as early as 1910, that small owners were numerous where the land lent itself to small-scale production, as in the overwhelmingly peasant villages of the Isle of Axholme, but were at a disadvantage where the essential condition of success was large capital expenditure as in the warp lands along the Trent.

It will be noticed, however, that all these examples are drawn from the predominantly arable areas. A typical example of enclosure in the pasture area is that of Queniborough, enclosed in 1794. Here a large part of the land had been converted to pasture, and the Reporter, a strong critic of enclosures, tells us that productivity was no greater in any department, no more corn nor cattle, nor increased produce of butter or cheese or beef. The output of grain remained about the same on a smaller acreage owing to an increase in yield by about 50–100 per cent; the sheep were fewer in number but were fed on green fodder crops and sold fat instead of lean; and there were far fewer losses from disease to which they were liable in the open fields. Indeed, he quotes a local farmer to the effect that the losses had been so heavy that there was some doubt whether the occupiers could have gone on in the open fields; and when we hear, as we do again and again, of flocks being halved or entirely swept away by sheep-rot on the undrained and disease-ridden commons, of the scourge of abortion among cattle on the commons, of the frequent outbreaks of cattle plague to which the Quarter Sessions Minute Books refer, we can well believe it. Our concern, however, is not with the mortality of sheep and cattle on the commons, but with that of peasants in the enclosed villages. In Queniborough there was no benevolent Duke of Rutland to temper the harsh winds to the shorn lamb; on the contrary there were two large owners who pressed their tenants hard by raising their rents from 12s. to 23s., greatly reduced the arable area and diminished the head of stock. Here we have all the circumstances that might be expected to result in a sharp decline of the small cultivator and to a reduction of population. But an examination of the enclosure

award and the land tax returns does not confirm this expectation. For ten years before and after enclosure there is no sign of change either in numbers of tenants or of owners or in amounts of tax paid; the names of the allottees at the enclosure recur in the land tax returns and remain substantially the same until about 1810 when new owners and tenants come in, possibly as a result of an invasion of the villages by stockingers to which the Agricultural Reporter had referred in 1809; and it may be that we must look to this source for the steady increase of population — 25 per cent between 1801–51 — which the census figures reveal. The number of farm tenancies seems to have declined somewhat, from twenty-four in 1790 (three years before enclosure) to twenty-one in 1810 and twenty in 1830 though there was an increase of very small tenancies which again may be due to stockinger influx.

But the case of Queniborough does not dispose of the problem of enclosure and depopulation in Leicestershire. The census returns show many cases of declining population during one or more of the census periods, an average in fact of between forty and fifty in each period. The responsibility of parliamentary enclosure for this result is, however, hard to establish, since most of the villages in question belong to the area of old enclosure, i.e. before 1700. Of the twenty-one villages enclosed by act of parliament after 1790, the census returns show some evidence of decline in ten, but all of them seem to belong to the area of stiff clay which was too heavy for mixed agriculture based on turnips. Like the Vale of Evesham, they seem to fall into the category of deep rich grazing grounds which lent themselves to permanent pasture. In villages such as these, enclosure was rounding off two centuries of adaptation to the special circumstances of the soil; but even here, where, as Dr. Hoskins has shown, the authentic voice of depopulation is unmistakably heard, the fall is far from catastrophic, the highest figure being the 24 per cent decline in Slawston between 1801–11, the others oscillating between 4 and 17 per cent, though they show a slight over-all increase in the period 1801–51.

Perhaps we may inquire at this stage what were the factors that tended to keep the rural population on the soil and indeed to increase it even where the opposite results might have been expected.

One important factor contributing to the stability of the agrarian population during this period was the high level of employment which was maintained both in enclosed and open parishes where the improved agriculture was adopted. The explanation seems to be that new agricultural practices had developed in advance of the technical devices for dealing with them. Thus the yield of corn per acre went up (e.g. at Queniborough from 50 to 100 per cent) after enclosure but the methods of ploughing, sowing, reaping and threshing were not substantially speeded up until the 1830's and 1840's. At the same time the spread of turnip cultivation and green fodder crops both in open and enclosed villages called for labour throughout the year in field, barn and stackyard; the maintenance of a milking herd or fatstock involved continuous field work throughout the year in pasture districts as well as arable, except where the land was too stiff for mixed farming as in south-east Leicestershire; and the hedging and ditching of the new enclosures found winter work for casual labour to a greater extent than the open villages. As for enclosure of forest, moor and fen, labour was attracted from far and wide.

In regard to parishes mainly given over to pasture like Queniborough and other Leicestershire parishes, we should remember that much of it was in convertible leys, i.e. an arable form of grass farming. William Marshall speaks of the grass lands of the old enclosures being subjected "to an alternacy of grass and arable the land having lain six or seven years in a state of sward, it is broken up for oats," then wheat and barley and then a further six years under grass; and mentions the practice of growing wheat on a clover ley even in the open fields. Moreover, in ley farming on heavy land, grass may take the place of turnips, so that although in many parishes in Leicestershire turnips were not grown, this need not imply that the new farming was unknown there. Indeed, I am told there are still parishes in Leicestershire where convertible leys are preferred to turnips owing to the high cost of producing them on heavy soil.

In regard to the numerical increase of cottage owners revealed by the land tax returns at a time when the most cautious authorities — e.g. Sir John Clapham and Professor Gonner — are of the opinion that they were stripped of their small properties, it should be remembered that in addition to the reasons given — the recognition of the claims of the smallest owners, who may have thus come into the land tax returns for the first time; the sale of land in small lots to pay expenses; the influx of purchasers from outside — there was also the stimulation of rural trades and industries as a result of the greater productivity of farming, the rise of population and the increasing traffic on the roads. The Agricultural Reporter for Leicestershire, in accounting for the maintenance of rural population in the Vale of Belvoir in spite of enclosure, speaks of the mechanics, blacksmiths, wheelwrights, tailors, weavers, who with the labourers and their families together may equal ten or twelve to every 100 acres. Moreover, the £5,000,000 or £6,000,000 spent in poor relief would represent a redistribution of rural incomes most of which, as the Hammonds do well to remind us, would find its way into the pockets of rural tradesmen who had an interest in supplying the pauperized labourers with the goods which they could have partly supplied, before enclosure, for themselves.

It will be seen, therefore, that the enclosure acts had the effect of further reducing, but not of destroying, the remaining English peasantry. They came at the end of a long period of attrition by consolidation and purchase and direct eviction which practically eliminated the peasantry from the parishes of old enclosure; but in the open villages, although there had been differentiation among the peasantry themselves, especially at the expense of the middle peasant, as well as attempts at consolidation by the landlord, the small owners and tenants were still remarkably strong. With the upward turn of rents in the 'fifties (of which accelerating enclosure was a symptom) there was further loss of tenants by consolidation and of owners by purchase; but when prices took their war-time leap and the attack on the waste got under way, there were gains of both as well as losses. What the net loss in farming units was it is not possible to calculate, but it was catastrophic only in particular localities; and where large areas of waste were involved or where conditions were especially favourable to small-scale cultivation, there was considerable increase in numbers. Professor Clapham has reminded us that the ratio of labouring families to farming families rose slowly, and that while it was 1.74 to 1 in Gregory King's time, it was still only 2½ to 1 in 1831. He concluded that "the Census figures are entirely destructive of the view, that as a result of agrarian change and class legislation, an army of labourers toiled for a relatively small farming class; we have not a proletarian army under officers"; . . . "numerically the average agricultural unit must be compared, not with the factory, but with handicraft workshops — master, journeyman or two, prentice or two."

Moreover, in view of the great amount of enclosure for pasture in the first half of the eighteenth century a large proportion of the fall in the number of farming units had occurred before the great era of parliamentary enclosures opened; "Sweet Auburn, loveliest village of the plain," the deserted village of Goldsmith's poetic imagination, was written in 1770, and had few if any authentic successors. Since the rural population in general was unmistakably on the increase during this time, the contribution which the dispossessed made to the industrial labour force came, in the majority of cases, from the unabsorbed surplus, not from the main body.

But to say this — and much else might be said in clarification of the statistical picture — is not to minimize the social consequences of the loss of the commons. The appropriation to their own exclusive use of practically the whole of the common waste by the legal owners meant that the curtain which separated the growing army of labourers from utter proletarianization was torn down. It was, no doubt, a thin and squalid curtain, for it will be remembered that Gregory King classed them all as actual or potential paupers who "decreased the wealth of the country"; but it was real, and to deprive them of it without providing a substitute implied the exclusion of the labourers from the benefits which their intensified labour alone made possible.

That this was a social calamity — brought into relief all the more by contrast with the contemporary land settlement in Denmark — may be conceded without admitting the measure of responsibility it is usually given for the recruitment of the reserve army of labour. As we have seen, the cottage-owning population seems actually to have increased after enclosure. Even the proletarianized labourers continued to remain on the soil in increasing numbers in most areas until the 1830's and in some parts to the 1840's, when improved farming techniques and railway transport caught up with the new farming practices. It was then that the real flight from the country-side began.

If agrarian change, as symbolized by enclosure, cannot be regarded as the chief recruiting agent of the industrial proletarian army, where did the new drafts come from which not only manned the expanding industries but the expanding agriculture also; and manned them in such strength that in some departments, the very plethora of labour was itself a brake upon techno logical innovation?

Economic historians are generally agreed that the fever of technical improvement in the early phases of the Industrial Revolution was partly occasioned by labour shortage even though enclosure was reported to be emptying the villages and bringing desolation to the countryside. What happened to transform the situation so that in the last quarter of the eighteenth century labour became available for an unprecedented expansion of industry and agriculture, for fighting a twenty years' war and for summoning up the grim spectre of the Malthusian population formula to the terror of statesmen who might otherwise have been prompted to remedial action? The only answer can be that at some unspecified time in the eighteenth century the movement of population had taken an upward turn in village and town alike and provided an entirely new supply of human material beside which the dislocations caused by enclosures were of secondary importance. The Isle of Axholme, an example unique in England, of a peasant community of the continental type, is a case in point. There was no question here of the institutional pressure of enclosure and the large farm. The inhabitants, small cultivators growing successive crops of corn, potatoes, hemp, flax, on their little farms of from four to fifty acres, with a few large ones of 200 or more, worked like negroes, says Arthur Young, and the smallest of them lived worse than the occupants of the poor house, but "all is made amends for by *possessing* land." An examination of the land tax returns shows that between 1783 and 1800 the numbers of freeholders rose from 829 to 1,326 an increase of 60 per cent; and between 1800 and 1829 to 1,444, a further increase of 9 per cent. But while the property owners were increasing by 9 per cent, in the same period the population went up by 33 per cent (from 7,214 to 9,626). Thus in this classically peasant region, the population rose faster than the units of property; a proletariat was coming into being by the natural increase of the peasant population. Moreover, it will be seen, by comparing the growth of these villages with the non-peasant villages around, that they grew in numbers side by

side with the landlord villages until the 1840's and then they diverged, the landlord villages showing a steady decline, the peasant villages going on for another two generations until they, too, began to falter in the teeth of the blizzard which blew up for farmers of all kinds in the last quarter of the century. The difference of institutional structure seems to have made no difference to the contribution made to the reserve army of labour: it may, for all we know, have been proportionally the same: no more and no less, until the second half of the century when the non-peasant villages entered on their numerical decline.

If it be conceded, as I think it must, that the period 1780–1840 saw only a sporadic exodus (apart from the migration of the surplus) from the rural areas which have formed the subject of this paper, and side by side with it, an actual filling up of empty spaces and a steady rise in the great majority of established centres of rural population, we are tempted to ask, from what hidden springs did this surge of rural population come, a surge that not only flowed over into what had formerly been empty and almost desert places — the black lings of Tideswell and Castleton, the heights of Mam Tor, and a score of sparsely occupied forests and marshes and yet had a surplus to spill over into the growing centres of industry in towns and industrialized villages? This phenomenon of rural fecundity is all the more remarkable since it follows a period marked by enclosure and the consolidation of farms on such a scale as to persuade many observers that the rural population was actually on the decline, being driven from their homes by the improving farmer and the rent-hungry landlord.

The remarkable paradox of visible population growth side by side with the lamentations of rural desolation engaged the attention, among others, of John Howlett and Arthur Young. Both agreed that in so far as enclosure was associated with capital investment in improved agriculture, it was followed not by a decline but by a growth of population. Arthur Young elaborates on this theme again and again and expounds, with a wealth of illustrations, the theory that an expanding economy will call into being its own labour supply by providing incentives to early marriage. In his *Northern Tour,* written in 1770, he says, "the only complaint he met with was the high price of agricultural labour, the causes of which he attributes to turnpikes, navigations, drainages and enclosures: all these conspired to make hands scarce and to depress the farmer." But he goes on:

It is employment that creates population: marriages are early and numerous in proportion to the amount of employment. In a great Kingdom there must always be hands that are idle, backward in the age of work, unmarried for fear of having families, or industrious only to a certain degree. Now an increase of employment raises wages and high wages changes the case of all these hands; the idle are converted to industry; the young come early to work; the unmarried are no longer fearful of families and the formerly industrious become so in a much greater degree. It is an absolute impossibility that in such circumstances the people should not increase. . . . Provide new employment and new hands will inevitably follow.

In more measured language, Adam Smith was writing in much the same strain and at the same time pointing out that "the real recompense of labour" had risen which "enabled them to provide for their children and consequently to bring up a greater number of them." Twenty years later, Eden and Malthus related population growth to the greatly increased demand for labour "combined with a greatly increased power of production, both in agriculture and manufactures."

Later historians have been inclined to look for the reason in the institutional factors of enclosures and poor law, which, they tell us, reduced the dispossessed peasantry to hopelessness and despair and removed the last remaining restraints upon "unbridled impulse." The regional historian has no competence to discuss these views in their wider implications, but he may be able to set them within the context of the local economy in so far as the special tools of his trade enable him to re-create it. In addition to those already used in this article there are others, such as marriage registers, estate accounts, testamentary inventories and the history of cottage architecture, together with the London prices — in the absence of local ones — of wheat and capital. By these means it may be possible to attempt a comparative study of regional demographic and secular trends during this crucial period of rural population growth.

A study of the marriage registers of 117 Nottinghamshire villages suggests that about the middle of the century the marriage rate took a decisive turn upwards, not only in the partially industrialized villages where the stocking industry and mining were entering on a phase of rapid expansion, but also in the agricultural villages, whether subject to enclosure or not. The rate of increase slowed down in the latter but accelerated in the former to the end of the century, but there seems to be no doubt that among the sources of the demographic revolution of the eighteenth century was the slow-moving but immensely powerful tide of agricultural change. Some light on the nature of this underswell is thrown by the movement of prices, rents, arrears, and farm vacancies on the Nottinghamshire estates of the Duke of Kingston. A comparison of this with the marriage trend suggests that about 1750 there was a simultaneous upward movement of the agricultural series and the marriage series after a period during which agriculture appears to have been depressed and marriages showed only a slight tendency to rise. Evidence of another kind — the widespread rebuilding of Midland farm houses in a solid brick and tile which survives today and the rising value and variety of testamentary inventories left by yeomen and husbandmen would suggest that agricultural investment and living standards were moving upwards in the region from the late seventeenth century in spite of the evidence of depression shown in the account books of the

Duke of Kingston. The low level of food prices in the 1730's might be expected to bring about a fall in the infant death rate which may be reflected in the rise in the marriage trend twenty years later, a rise which the general expansion from the 1750's would sustain. With the slight upward turn from 1750 of rents and prices, the fall in rent arrears and farm vacancies, the expansion of industry in the rural and urban centres, together with the maintenance of low interest rates, the context for a parallel movement in the secular curve of prosperity and population was complete, and the conditions for an adequate labour supply were at last fulfilled.

Whether this inference will bear the test of wider inquiry remains to be seen, but the evidence is such as to cast doubt on the *a priori* assumption that the reserve army of labour was an "institutional creation" in the sense of being a response to the exercise of power by a ruling class; it may also be seen as the outcome of the complex of forces represented by an expanding economy which offered inducements as well as compulsions, e.g. to inventors to supplement the labour force and to parents to augment it, while making possible for their offspring a more favourable chance of survival than had ever before been known. A demographic change was thus set in motion which itself became a fact of history, and has to be taken account of if a balanced picture is to be drawn of the social stresses of the time; and in a recognition of this lies the best hope of reconciling the apparent inconsistencies of the sociological and the economic approach with which this article began.

THE INDUSTRIAL REVOLUTION: A Reappraisal

GEORGE N. CLARK

G. N. Clark spent a few years as Professor of History at Cambridge, but most of his life he has taught at Oxford, where he is now Provost of Oriel College. He has specialized in the seventeenth century, and his books *The Seventeenth Century* and the volume on the period 1660–1714 in *The Oxford History of England* show that he has ranged far beyond economic topics. In this lecture, he sums up the views of a lifetime of scholarship in characteristically temperate language.

Soon after the end of the first German war, a number of tendencies at work in the British universities converged to produce a remarkable activity in historical research. The pre-occupations of the time were such that recent economic and social history was one of the departments where this activity was greatest. The amount of detailed information about it available to historians was multiplied many times. There were many books and innumerable articles on special industries or localities or processes. New kinds of material were used, especially business archives, the actual records of factories, mines, banks, farms and shops. At first the line of approach was, like Toynbee's, from the social concern with economic conditions. Under the guidance of a few leading historians new schools of interpretation grew up, sympathetic to the earlier nineteenth-century liberalism which collectivism had deflected from its course. As the monographs accumulated they gradually effected a revision of the accepted version of the story; a revision after the approved scientific pattern in which premature generalizations succumb to the onset of new facts. At the same time the new facts and the old came to be regarded from new points of view. Historians of the labour and socialist movements

appeared, some of whom saw them from the outside and identified themselves, like Green and Toynbee, with society as a whole while others saw them from the inside and thought that, whether society was a whole or not, the cause of the workers was a reality with its own history. Another set of investigators, almost independently, pressed on with the history of technology, and they joined hands with the historians of science. I must mention with proper humility Professor Lancelot Hogben's inaugural lecture of 1937 on *The Theoretical Leadership of Scottish Science in the English Industrial Revolution.*

It lies beyond my present purpose to survey the results of all this activity or to summarize the conclusions which it justifies about the course of history. I am concerned only with the central question, what effect it has had on the idea of the Industrial Revolution. To begin with, I need hardly say, it has broadened and deepened and sharpened our knowledge so much that many puzzles have been sorted out, and many problems solved. Like all explaining it has its disappointing side: it has smoothed away the contrasts and surprises, the exceptions and the discontinuities. When the sequence of the great inventions was studied in its full social context, the late

From George N. Clark, *The Idea of the Industrial Revolution* (Jackson, Son & Co., Ltd., Glasgow, 1953), pp. 26–33. (This selection is an extract from the Twentieth Lecture on the David Murray Foundation in the University of Glasgow, delivered on October 15, 1952.)

eighteenth century ceased to look like a new beginning. Each step was found to have been prepared for by many antecedent conditions. Mechanization was a response to market-requirements; its pace and range were determined by the state of scientific knowledge and the available skilled industrial manpower. No one industry, no one locality had an entirely separate history of its own but none went forward exactly in step with the others. There were factories and wholly urban industries before the cotton-mills. When the relevant factors in commerce, in policy, in finance, in the metal-industries, were considered, it proved to be necessary to go back at least as far as the late seventeenth century if the story of the Industrial Revolution was to be told without beginning in the middle. The revolution was dissolved into the aggregate of countless changes, large and small, spread over a long period of time. No wonder historians mislike the phrase: to talk about a revolution which began in the seventeenth century and is unfinished in the twentieth is making very free with words.

From the chronological point of view the idea of the Industrial Revolution has collapsed. It must indeed be conceded that the short period to which the name used to be given was a period of rapid change. Research has not shown that Robert Owen and John Galt and Sir Walter Scott were incapable of using their eyes. There *were* wonderful new machines; there *was* a great growth and displacement of population; there *was* a new kind of social discontent. But these were not aspects of one unique mutation in economic life which can be summed up in a formula of a single sentence. In particular, the formula of Arnold Toynbee, the substitution of competition for medieval regulations, seems now to have little or no value. Toynbee, like many other English historians, did not compare our history with that of other countries. If he had done so he would have seen what we cannot fail to see after the world's subsequent experience, that the industrializing process has often occurred without any such substitution. Precisely because indus-

trialized Britain was strong enough to invade every market in the name of free trade, other countries deliberately industrialized themselves under the shelter of protectionism, and it was in pursuit of this end that the extremes of state-control were reached. Even if we leave this foreign comparison out of account, we can no longer accept Toynbee's view of the English past. The period before 1760 was more competitive than he allowed. Many of the social evils which aroused his indignation had festered for centuries. Research has done much since Toynbee's time in exploring the horrible records of child-labour, excessive hours, bad housing, malnutrition and epidemics in England before 1760. He was excusably misled into exaggerating their novelty by the scarcity of the information available to him; but it was a radical defect of his method which led him to relate them as he did to the principle of *laissez-faire*.

Between 1760 and 1846 many time-honoured, if ineffective, legislative restrictions on economic enterprise were done away with. Such were wage-regulations, usury laws, restraints on joint-stock enterprise, and Toynbee explained this as the application of the principle of which *laissez-faire* was the slogan. He recognized that there were some contrary changes, though I think he included in this class only the early factory laws. He did not notice, as Dicey did, how drastically the state overrode the rights of property in the social interest when it imposed taxation or when it made laws for the building of roads, canals, railways, and docks. In the special field of public finance Professor D. H. Macgregor in a pregnant little book which was unfortunately published during the recent war, *"Public Aspects of Finance"* (1939), has demolished Toynbee's view of the first phase of "the liberal plan of capitalist democracy." "It is not true," he tells us, "that planning must always imply, far less be defined by, an increased degree of interference of restriction." In his view, *laissez-faire* was part of a plan. This is true not only in public finance but in the whole of social policy. *Laissez-faire* was not a passport given by an indifferent state to ruthless enterprise; it was a demand made by energy and common sense when they found themselves obstructed. *"Laissez faire, laissez passer"* means not, as some people imagine, "let it be" or "let us be," but "let us act, let us by, get out of our way." The policy which it expressed was adopted not only because it enabled merchants and manufacturers to make fortunes without regard to the needs of the wage-earners; but because it opened the gates for the new wealth without which there could have been no social welfare. By the time of Green and Toynbee that stage of social reform was nearing its completion, and the next stage needed a new plan of control and interference. Like some other writers of their time in England and on the Continent who came to history for the answer to questionings which originated in the sphere of religion, they seemed to suppose that thinkers in their studies excogitate ideas which then impinge on social life from outside. Thus they ignored the intricate interdependences of eighteenth-century social, economic, political and intellectual history, tracing back the origin of social evils to fallacious economics and hoping for a remedy from a change of mind.

This was a defect of method, and patient research has undone the mischief, but many of the more recent writers on the Industrial Revolution have made similar and perhaps less venial mistakes. The idealist fallacy in historiography is only one example of the error of seeking for a prime mover in history. Another, or something very much like it, is the tendency to magnify the importance of a single factor. One good historian gives the impression that things would have gone on much the same throughout the eighteenth century if it had not been for the enormous growth of international commerce. That conclusion, no doubt, was better than ascribing all the changes to a few mechanical inventions; but it was only one facet of the many-sided truth. The same may be said of the emphasizing of the part played by demand or by

the rate of interest in multiplying production. It may be said also of the contention, favoured at the present time when demographic studies are so active, that the growth of population was a great primary datum in the age of cotton and steam.

If we consider how this perpetual bias towards magnifying the importance of some single factor has distorted thought about social and economic history, we may turn back to the idea of the Industrial Revolution in an indulgent frame of mind. In comparison with most recent work, it is indeed clumsy, crude and misleading. It is not susceptible of statistical proof; it did not emerge from a comprehensive scrutiny of manuscript sources; it owes nothing to any kind of scientific technique. But it is still worth keeping alive and not only as a title for books which are really about something else. There is no harm in using it in that way. It is a handy phrase for describing a period, or giving a preliminary notion of the relation between that period and some other. But we can make a better use of it. It has rendered and it can still render a great and necessary service, the service, if I may express it so, of confusing people's minds. To overlook all factors except one is to think abstractly without intending it. Economic history is an abstract kind of history, tracing the chain of one kind of causes and effects to the exclusion of all the factors which are not economic. Like all abstract historical study, it ought to end, as it began, with the concrete. This is true of both its substance and its terminology. "Industrial Revolution" was once a phrase of two abstract words; but by use it has acquired almost as much nature as a proper name. We write it with capital letters. Now a proper name has the virtue that we cannot escape from its emotional associations. They recall us from decontaminated abstractions to concrete human life, and they remind us that the concrete cannot be expressed in formulae. As matter for research it is inexhaustible; but it is not unapproachable. We have access to it through ideas like the idea of the Industrial Revolution.

SUGGESTIONS FOR ADDITIONAL READING[1]

Useful background books on the Industrial Revolution are Herbert Heaton, *Economic History of Europe* (1936 and later editions), which covers a long period but always with precision; Charles R. Fay, *Great Britain from Adam Smith to the Present Day* (1928 and later editions); William H. B. Court, *A Concise Economic History of Britain from 1750 to Recent Times* (Cambridge, 1954); while a shorter treatment of problems dealt with in the present book is Henry L. Beales, *The Industrial Revolution, 1750–1850, an Introductory Essay* (1928).

Additional material for estimating industrialization in Britain before 1750 is in Ephraim Lipson, *An Economic History of England* (1931 and later editions), Vols. II and III; Henry Hamilton, *The English Brass and Copper Industries to 1800* (1926); Alfred P. Wadsworth and Julia de L. Mann, *The Cotton Trade and Industrial Lancashire, 1600–1780* (Manchester, 1931); and John U. Nef, *The Growth of the British Coal Industry* (2 vols., 1932).

The Hammonds have dealt, in more detail but in the same way, with workers' conditions in, *The Town Labourer, 1760–1832, The New Civilization* (1918); *The Skilled Labourer, 1760–1832* (1919); and *The Age of the Chartists, 1832–54* (1930); while J. L. Hammond answered critics in an article "The Industrial Revolution and Discontent," *Economic History Review*, II, No. 2 (1930), pp. 215–28. Further detail on social conditions, from a somewhat similar point of view, can be found in George D. H. Cole, *A Short History of the British Working Class Movement 1789–1947* (use the 1948 edition); B. L. Hutchins and A. Harrison, *A History of Factory Legislation* (1903); Mark Hovell, *The Chartist Movement* (Manchester, 1918); Ivy Pinchbeck,

Women Workers and the Industrial Revolution (1930); while on trade unions the standard work is still Sidney and Beatrice Webb (sometimes catalogued under their later title of Passfield), *History of Trade Unionism* (1894, and a revised edition, 1920); the many more modern works amplify and correct this single great book.

Against this view, Thomas S. Ashton has argued, in more technical detail than in the excerpts chosen for this book, in "The Standard of Life of the Workers in England, 1790–1830," *Journal of Economic History*, IX (1949), Supplement, pp. 19–38, but reprinted in Hayek, *Capitalism and the Historians.* (1954) He makes use of Elizabeth W. Gilboy, *Wages in Eighteenth Century England* (Cambridge, Mass., 1934), while admitting that all eighteenth century statistics are imperfect. Note also J. H. Clapham, *An Economic History of Modern Britain,* Vol. I (Cambridge, 1926), Chapter 14.

Since the present book was compiled, a restatement of the "pessimistic" view of the Industrial Revolution's social consequences has been advanced, with much new information as well as new arguments: Eric J. Hobsbawm, "The British Standard of Living, 1790–1850," *Economic History Review*, Second Series, X (1957), 46–61.

A view similar to Mantoux's on the fate of the small landowner and laborer after enclosure, but more colorfully stated, is John L. and Barbara Hammond, *The Village Labourer, 1760–1832, A Study in the Government of England before the Reform Bill* (1911). Somewhat more favorable to enclosure is Rowland E. Prothero (Lord Ernle), *English Farming Past and Present* (1912 and later editions). Much more favorable is the highly technical Edmund C. K. Gonner, *Common Land and Inclosure* (1912). Another detailed discussion is in W. H. R. Curtler, *The Enclosure and Redistribution of Our Land* (Oxford, 1920).

[1] Unless otherwise stated, the place of publication is London.

New evidence is used in E. Davies, "The Small Landowner, 1780–1832, in the Light of the Land Tax Assessments," *Economic History Review,* I, No. 1 (1927), pp. 87–113; and in Jonathan D. Chambers, "Enclosure and the Small Landowner," *ibid.,* X, No. 2 (1940), pp. 118–27. Detailed studies of the personnel of the Commissioners are Maurice W. Beresford, "Commissioners of Enclosure," *ibid.,* XVI, No. 2 (1946), pp. 130–40; and W. E. Tate, "Oxfordshire Enclosure Commissioners, 1737–1856," *Journal of Modern History,* XXIII (1951), pp. 137–45.

Studies of firms and industries have shown how many of the hardships of the early industrialization can be explained, if not justified, in terms of the difficulties of industrialists in the face of shortage of capital and acute competition, with no support from paternal government and little from trade associations. Perhaps the best are the following. George Unwin, *Samuel Oldknow and the Arkwrights* (Manchester, 1924); George W. Daniels, *The Early English Cotton Industry* (1920); William B. Crump, *The Leeds Woollen Industry, 1780–1820* (Leeds, 1931); Thomas S. Ashton, *Iron and Steel in the Industrial Revolution* (1924); A. Raistrick, *A Dynasty of Ironfounders, the Darbys of Coalbrookdale* (1953); Thomas S. Ashton, *An Eighteenth Century Industrialist, Peter Stubs of Warrington* (Manchester, 1939); Archibald and N. Clow, *The Chemical Revolution* (1932); Thomas S. Ashton and J. Sykes, *The English Coal Industry of the Eighteenth Century* (Manchester, 1929); John Lord, *Capital and Steam Power, 1750–1800* (1923); and Erich Roll, *An Early Experiment in Industrial Organization, . . . The Firm of Boulton and Watt, 1775–1805* (1930).

Studies of towns and regions are also adding much to our understanding of the process of industrialization. Among the best are the following, but any list is likely to be out of date as soon as it is written. Henry Hamilton, *The Industrial Revolution in Scotland* (Oxford, 1932); E. R. R. Green, *The Lagan Valley, 1800–50, A Local History of the Industrial Revolution* (1949); Arthur H. Dodd, *The Industrial Revolution in North Wales* (Cardiff, 1933); Arthur H. John, *The Industrial Development of South Wales, 1750–1850* (Cardiff, 1950); William H. B. Court, *The Rise of the Midland Industries, 1600–1838* (1938); Jonathan D. Chambers, *Nottinghamshire in the Eighteenth Century* (1932); William J. Rowe, *Cornwall in the Age of the Industrial Revolution* (Liverpool, 1953); M. Dorothy George, *London Life in the Eighteenth Century* (1926); Arthur Redford, *Manchester Merchants and Foreign Trade, 1794–1858* (Manchester, 1934); Conrad Gill and Asa Briggs, *History of Birmingham* (2 vols., 1952); William H. Chaloner, *The Social and Economic Development of Crewe* (Manchester, 1950); Theodore C. Barker and J. R. Harris, *A Merseyside Town in the Industrial Revolution, St. Helens, 1750–1900* (Liverpool, 1954); Charles R. Fay, *Round About Industrial Britain, 1830–60* (Toronto, 1952).

Further technical studies written by economists include: Walther Hoffmann, *British Industry 1700–1950* (English Translation, Oxford, 1955: the German first edition was 1939); Werner Schlote, *British Overseas Trade, from 1700 to the 1930's* (English translation, Oxford, 1952: German edition, 1938); but above all, for the modern economic approach, but written with easy grace, Thomas S. Ashton, *An Economic History of England, The Eighteenth Century* (1955).

On the population problem, not dealt with in the present book, see especially G. Talbot Griffith, *Population Problems in the Age of Malthus* (Cambridge, 1926); Mabel C. Buer, *Health, Wealth and Population in the Early Days of the Industrial Revolution* (1926); Arthur Redford, *Labour Migration in England, 1800–50* (Manchester, 1926); Kenneth H. Connell, *The Population of Ireland, 1750–1845* (Oxford, 1950); T. H. Marshall, "The Population Problem during the Industrial Revolution," *Eco-*

nomic Journal (*Economic History* Series, No. 4, January 1929), pp. 429–56; H. J. Habbakuk, "English Population in the Eighteenth Century," *Economic History Review,* Second Series, VI, No. 2 (1953), pp. 117–33.

Information on personalities referred to in the excerpts or in additional reading may often be found in *The Dictionary of National Biography.* To keep up-to-date, consult articles and book reviews in *Journal of Economic History, Journal of Political Economy, Economic Journal,* and, above all, *Economic History Review.*